ordinary losses
naming the graces that shape us

Elisa Stanford

PARACLETE PRESS
Brewster, Massachusetts

Library of Congress Cataloging-in-Publication Data
  Stanford, Elisa Fryling.
  Ordinary losses : naming the graces that shape us / Elisa Fryling Stanford.
     p. cm.
  ISBN 1-55725-403-6 (trade paper)
  1. Stanford, Elisa Fryling. 2. Young adults—Religious life. 3. Loss
(Psychology)—Religious aspects—Christianity. I. Title.
  BV4529.2.S73 2004
  242—dc22   2004013662

10 9 8 7 6 5 4 3 2 1

© 2004 by Elisa Fryling Stanford

ISBN 1-55725-403-6

Published by Paraclete Press
Brewster, Massachusetts
www.paracletepress.com

Printed in the United States of America.

for my parents
with gratitude

CONTENTS

FOREWORD ix

INTRODUCTION xi

CHAPTER ONE

All I Can Remember: Home 1

CHAPTER TWO

When Every Light Meant Home: Peace 9

CHAPTER THREE

All That Might Be: Hope 20

CHAPTER FOUR

Between the Mysteries: Wonder 33

CHAPTER FIVE

Pieces of Ourselves: Relationship 43

CHAPTER SIX

The Missing Hours: Time and Opportunity 56

CHAPTER SEVEN

Jumping In: Courage 66

CHAPTER EIGHT

One Thing: Passion   77

CHAPTER NINE

First Words: Voice   90

CHAPTER TEN

My True Name: Identity   102

CHAPTER ELEVEN

And Heaven to Earth Will Answer: God   113

ACKNOWLEDGMENTS   123

ENDNOTES   125 by Lauren F. Winner

The manuscript of Elisa Fryling Stanford's small book found me at just the right time. This book, as the title tells us, is about ordinary losses, and in the few months before Elisa's book came to me I had experienced two losses that were very ordinary and very extraordinary—my mother died and I got married. *Getting married is a loss,* you might be wondering. *I thought it was a definite gain!* And it is a gain, but imagine, or remember back, to the ordinary things that are lost when you marry—nights alone, the potential for a wider path, and spinster fantasies; I find dying to my fantasies of being a spinster in some cold New England clime a particularly hard loss.

I wasn't sure, actually, that I wanted to read another book about loss. I'd already gone through C. S. Lewis's *A Grief Observed,* and a book on motherless daughters, and even an ethnography of Jewish bereavement customs. I was ready now for something more uplifting: Agatha Christie, or a return to Jane Austen. Or perhaps I needed to take a break from books altogether and learn to knit.

But by the second chapter of Elisa's book I was grateful to have found *Ordinary Losses.* It is not a book about big, horrible losses. *Ordinary Losses* is instead about the unspeakable absence we feel at the oddest times: in the middle of a bright summer afternoon, when just for a moment the world feels like the saddest thing ever; or when we bounce a baby on our knee and are suddenly pierced through by the ending of our own childhood; or when we look down our street and around our town and know that we have no idea what pain and suffering go on inside the sweet brick houses that make up our neighborhood.

Ordinary Losses cultivates the sense that something is not quite right, here; that something is missing; that something will be missing until we reach eternity. It places us in the topography of in-between and not-yet, the Christian posture of anticipation. It is, finally, about Advent, about expectation, and it is good company for those of us, pilgrims, who are called to wait.

At night before sleep, my sister and I tossed words to each other, one saying a word and the other responding with the first word that came into her mind: *Straw* led to *hay* led to *farm* led to *barn* led to *red,* back and forth across the beds until the images in our minds were far from where we had started. When one of us called "reverse," we went back through where we'd been, trying to remember what made us think of *red,* what made us say *barn.* We won the game when we arrived at the first word without missing any words along the way and without being silenced by a parent from the hallway.

Perhaps this is also how we find our way home from loss, going back through the stories we've dropped behind us like words as we've lived. We trace through what we know to find who we are—to find the word that first started us.

We often think of loss as belonging to later life, but in truth loss shapes us from the time we are born. We lose, without being asked, our safety, our silence, our trust. We lose the earliest forms of our helplessness, our hunger, our thrashing wishes. Many of these losses are celebrated, as change thrusts us through, but in some slivers of time—waking in the night, feeling Christmas come, eyeing the anger of a friend—we sense that much is incomplete, much is yet to come. We realize that sometimes the greatest griefs are for what we never had.

※

I have always been tender toward what never was or never will be. I experience mornings, conversations, prayers in the space of what is missing, often feeling what is absent more than what is present. Yet the incompleteness offers hope, offers a longing that shapes itself to what might still be.

As a college student I discovered a Bible passage in the book of Ezra that named for me my own rhythm of joy and grief. As the Israelites rebuilt the temple that had been destroyed, "all the people gave a great shout of praise to the LORD." But many of the older people who had seen the former temple "wept aloud when they saw the foundation of this temple being laid." In the pulse of emotion surrounding the new foundation, "no one could distinguish the sound of the shouts of joy from the sound of weeping, because the people made so much noise. And the sound was heard far away."

I am young to great sorrows, to the wisdom and history that magnified the older Israelites' grief. But I love this passage because my life is full of shouts of joy as well as weeping, and the noise is great and indistinguishable in my soul. Every day is filled with both tearing down and building up. Pain and joy press in on me like ice and fire, each feeling twinges of the other, and to understand the fullness of both, I need to name them.

This book is about recognizing the losses that tear down so that more life might be built. It is about forming a faith out of hymns and onion-paper pages and then wondering, in an unexpected moment during a worship service, if God is worth trusting. It is about watching a friendship, once birthed in an unknown cave of beginnings, slip into the waters without a grasp to save it. It is about the catch in the soul when the sun slants toward us on an ordinary afternoon and it feels so new we wonder how long ago we last felt it.

These are the losses we never bury and rarely mourn—the absences that grow so slowly we barely notice the void they leave. We remember them out of order, if at all, and when we piece them together, we see ourselves. As memory and hope build and fall "no one could distinguish the sound of the shouts of joy from the sound of weeping."

⧴⧵

This book, these stories, are about the past, or how I dream the past might have been. It is about what I long for and want to create, what I remember once hoping for when promises were real, just beyond my vision.

It is through loss that we become hardened to childlikeness and through loss that we return again to childhood stories, to the imagination that lets one word lead to another. This is grace, to allow the same cry that tears us down to bring life.

In the end, I will stand in the silence of what once spoke so loudly. There I will hear, like a word whispered before sleep, my secret, wild name.

CHAPTER ONE

All I Can Remember: Home

One of my first experiences will also be one of my last: I am waiting for home. It was the summer of my fourth birthday, and I had requested a purple cake with orange roses. I asked my parents every day when this cake would come, and also when we would pack our car and drive away from our New Hampshire house, as I had been told we would. I understood that these events would happen close together and that I had to be patient.

Did I know for weeks or for months that we would be going to live in Wisconsin? Each day was a wide expanse of waiting; I saw no reason why we couldn't leave right now. "Are we moving today?" is one of the first things I remember saying—the question muddled now in my mind with an image of purple icing.

When we finally got into our station wagon and drove west, it may have been before or after my birthday. I remember the cake, the way the roses melted into the smear of the other frosting, but whether I picture the cake itself or my wanting of it, I don't know. In any case, I was relieved when the day of travel came. I did not know enough to be attached to a building or a people, I did not have a school to visit one more time. All distance was the same to me, so I observed my family's grief at the move with curiosity—I had no vocabulary for good-bye.

This would change in the land to which we traveled. If my questions in New Hampshire were the murmurings of a dream, the moment I discovered memory rooted in time was in the back of our station wagon—the "way back" we called it, perhaps all families did—hiding between our suitcases as my dad pulled up to a gas station. My mother was tired and my sister quiet, the windows of our car open to sticky June air. When my dad got back in the car, we drove the remaining mile to our new house. There I would learn that life can be more waiting than celebration, but that it is always a cadence of both, and that we are made to love a home so much we never want to leave it.

Anyone who has roots in New England carries for a lifetime a love for New England trees. Even I, who remember little more than the color of the carpets in our old house, miss the canopy of trees over me along the tight roads of New Hampshire, the way the year swivels on October weeks of reddening glory. So when our first fall in Madison rose brown and dry, my parents were reminded of where we were not, reminded that home is a long wait. When my mom noticed a patch of maples off the beltline, the first trees to turn that year, she pointed them out every time we drove past. Soon the rest of the city spoke of patched color. We trampled orange on the way to school, watched green turn rust, even red, even yellow that bowed to a lake we learned was the size of the Sea of Galilee.

Those trees by the beltline were the first to turn every year. A chain-link fence held them back from us, but still they were colored, still they assured that God will offer life for the beauty of it. To my mom those trees were the first sign that where we were was becoming home.

My parents, who grew up, met, and married on the East Coast, continued to talk about New England with fondness. I tried to picture them somewhere other than with me, but their past seemed a dim and tender fog. In my mind, our house in Madison was where life happened. All that went on before was a build-up to right now, and all that would happen after was too far away to believe.

When I went away to college, I decided with a desperate missing that home was where my family lived, wherever that was. On the way back to Madison at the end of my junior year, I talked so long and hard to my parents that I literally lost my voice. Home was where I could let out all my words.

When does *staying* become home, part of an unconscious list of things we can count on? My parents moved to another city soon after I graduated from college, and my childhood roots were flung open and raw, as the house I grew up in became the possession of someone who had no memory of it.

Even my most sensitive friends couldn't understand why I felt displaced, but others, like my tough Italian neighbor, melted when I lamented the move. "Aw, that's hard," Paul told me with a toothpick in his mouth and arms folded across his chest. "My parents sold my childhood house a few years ago, and, man, it was tough." He shook his head, remembering.

As my parents settled into a new house, I fell into a restless season. In my basement apartment I realized that we can live years in a place without ever coming home to it. I did not change the curtains, I did not hang pictures. *I am in-between, I will not stay here. I am ready to go.*

Now I live where trees themselves—not just colored leaves—are scarce. God is generous in where He places color, and Colorado finds almost all its color in the sky. For a brief week or two in the fall, though, the aspens turn, and the state population scurries to the high country with SUVs and water bottles. Driving up mountain roads, we hear the leaves pour themselves like silent gold. And so this, too, is home.

At a business lunch recently, I asked someone where he was from. "Well, I've lived in San Diego for ten years, which is longer than I've lived anywhere else. I'm starting to say I'm from there. I guess it's home." *I live here, but I'm not at home here,* we seem to say. *I want you to know that this is not the place I will always be, and it is definitely not the place where I began to become someone.* The question itself is revealing. "Where are you from?" means "Where did you become who you are? What made you choose to leave or stay?"

Now I search for the rootedness I knew as I wove my bike through neighborhood streets and explored backyard bushes without fear. I want to hide again between suitcases while someone strong carries me down new roads and assures me I will soon know them. Instead I plant my garden and marry and have children and hang sacred pictures on walls I'm told are mine, but I know that I will be leaving soon for sturdier shelters. I lean toward the leaving; I wait for it as my feet sink into the ground beneath me.

For though I did find home here, red-rock bright, I still feel the need to tell people that I come from somewhere else. I speak of past homes, reminding myself of what land has shaped me and telling myself that I can return to that place. Perhaps speaking of the past is acknowledging that God will one day bring me again to a place I know. So I live between the just-coming-from and the just-going-to, and I reach forward every morning in case a new, truer home should appear.

Since I've had my own home, I've thought more about Jesus' words, "I go to prepare a place for you." As I put out towels and think of what guests would like to eat, I realize that this is what my mom has done for years, readying a place in the shadow of the preparation Jesus does for us. I think of the times she got the house ready for my sister or for me to come home from college, from trips, from first years of marriage or motherhood. She prepared for us out of what she knew of us, and she delighted to prepare.

I think of friends who create homes for me, not just in their physical houses but in their conversation and questions. *I have prepared a place for you in this friendship; I have set the table and I'm ready for you to come sit by me.* I discover the presence of relational homes, homes that can bend as we move spiritually and geographically. I see this in my expanding family, understanding that we will never be able to fit in a Ford station wagon again.

Last year I traveled back East to visit my grandparents for the first time in several years. They live in a retirement community in Pennsylvania, not far from the row house where they made their home for almost fifty years of marriage. The sky reminds me of spring breaks with them, Easter mornings scrambling down their living room stairs.

On my second morning there, my friend Miriam, who lives in the area, gave me a ride to my grandparents' home. Miriam lives in the house her grandfather built fifty years ago. Her little-girl house was once surrounded by forty acres of family property. Now most of the property has been sold off and other houses have risen up around what is left. The house stands, but the home is being threatened.

Miriam tells me, as we drive through small Pennsylvania towns, that one Saturday that spring her family had an "arbor day." They planted five trees—pear trees and poplars, already seven or eight feet tall. The trees line one side of the house; later arbor days will fill in more space. Her family works to surround themselves with beauty; to let life take care of what time takes away.

I think of this as I watch the land around me, my grand-parents' and great-grandparents' land, my dad's land. Later, I will watch my grandmother take my grandfather's hand, as she has at many dinner tables, for evening walks, for thousands of prayers. I will watch my grandfather smile when she speaks, though his eyes cannot see her anymore. And I too want to plant trees around me. Trees that say, *This is where I come from. From this land anything can grow.*

⸻⸻⋈⸻⸻

Every fall my husband and I hike up to "The Crags," about an hour from our house. The path is not long, but it is steep in places, and every time we hike there, I think I'm not going to make it to the top. The walk takes us through a mix of forest and prairie, and we stop often to rest at well-placed logs. The last push to the top is barren, a sharp incline of stone leading to a reward of flat boulders and a giant view of the world. We sit and feel our bodies more fully than we did before the climb, spray water down our throats and quiet our breathing.

We are near the treeline, so most of the life around us is an enduring brown and green. Only the aspens we can see below are bright. In front of us, the sky is tall against the land. If we turn around, we see the rest of the mountain—the strength of all we will not climb—made up of evergreens reaching straight out of their rocky beds.

After one of our walks, when we turn back to the face of the mountain, we see an aspen in the midst of the pine above us. A shock of yellow among the darkness. "It's just up there, doin' its thing," a hiker next to me says.

As we start back down the mountain, I think of how in a few days or a few weeks that aspen's leaves will fall and feathery branches will highlight the green around them. Not many people will even notice the tree is standing. I think about how I enjoy knowing one path up one mountain in this state and what aspens look like in winter—more than I knew three years ago. I also enjoy carrying New Hampshire autumns, though they somehow slip away when I try to remember the shape of the leaves in our yard. I look again at the aspen higher and higher above me and let the yellow remind me of my mom driving past her beltline of trees and of the way color is one of the first things we know. I feel strong rock hold up my feet as I watch a single tree that has found its home reach for sky.

CHAPTER TWO

When Every Light
Meant Home: *Peace*

Morning against morning, I dream I am in my childhood bedroom. Behind my eyes, the room is yellow and tight,
with sharp corners on walls and furniture. As I sink into
today's reality, my yellow room dissipates and I find myself
adjusting to the light of another home. Edges slope to grays
and blues outside my window, an expanse of cement and
prairie. In this new land I hang on with tiny feet, remember in
a dream what it was like to wake to a day that was safe.

I am not disappointed to have traveled here, not saddened by the room in which I wake up, but still I scramble to move back to a childhood peace, distant and vivid as a dream. A friend recently pointed out to me how often I pray for peace. It is sometimes all I know to pray for. *Peace to you. May she have peace. Lord, I pray for peace.* We are paralyzed with disquiet, worry, fear, ambition. We are far from a child's waking and we long to return. So I pray for peace for myself, for others, for our mornings and our journeys home. I pray we will recognize the untamed peace of God. It may be the greatest dream we know.

❦

I wake again to Madison, to childhood. I chew memory like snow, feel it cold, melted, sharp. I always begin at our house, on the corner of Whitcomb Drive and Hammersley Road. Whitcomb was the street that I bravely crossed to look at the other side of the leaves on the corner tree, and Hammersley was the street that I never crossed because it was "busy," the word that spoke of all the ills and dangers in the world.

I float down Hammersley, under the archway of trees, turn right, find Whitney, and then Odana. Memory leaps to high school and West Towne Mall, landmarks rising in my mind like a cartoon drawing of hometown essentials— my dad's office, the arcade, the pet store, Lane's bakery.

The other side of Odana leads to Segoe, which winds through residential neighborhoods, past a school and several churches. It was Segoe that my elementary Sunday school teacher said was hard to navigate when she was learning to drive as an adult. My mom told me this as we practiced driving in high school. I tried to grasp the idea of Mrs. Wrobbel not being able to drive, since all adults seemed to have that ability.

Segoe leads to the bookstore where I worked on Wednesday evenings and Saturdays once I got my own license, where I closed out the registers at night with my eyes tired from piano lessons and homework, where my soul felt the richest peace it knew in high school as I opened the doors and turned on the music Saturday mornings. When I had no customers, I slid a book from the shelf and hid myself on the stool behind the counter, feeling the sun come in the large windows that held off insecurities for a few hours every week.

Driving home I thought of how my mom used to chuckle because the road was fairly straight after all—a twinge of the wrist to slide past a park or a baseball field. I pictured Mrs. Wrobbel with her hands on the ten and the two of the wheel, curving her car around this bending promise of a street.

Segoe leads to University, a street I did not like to drive, and if I carry University far enough in my mind, it drops off somewhere near the lake, near my high school church with Jesus standing tall over the door, his arms at his side and his hands open. "The shrugging Jesus," the downtown neighborhood called him. From this Jesus, a vague recess of side streets and small restaurants would lead back to my house if I could remember how they connected.

Streets going the other direction from Hammersley lead to Meadowridge Library, where I got my first library card, moving my head from side to side as I waited for the card to be laminated because I wanted my hair to bounce like Katie Sheldon's. On other visits, I played with the marble game in the corner before taking the swollen paperbacks of Judy Blume, *Little House in the Big Woods,* Choose-Your-Own-Adventure off the shelves.

Those streets around my home are grounded and friendly in my mind. In elementary school, I explored them afternoon to summer afternoon on my bike, or criss-crossed them on foot with my best friend, Emily, when we roamed through garage sales and came home with, each, a poster of fourteen brown puppies in a basket.

If I traveled farther from home, I would reach Sequoya Library, a blue memory, with high ceilings over growing girls sorting through its thready hardcovers. Sequoya held the research papers and dusty books that my mom and I looked up on weekends before my deadlines in junior high. The wooden clunk of the card catalog, the soft cards with numbers that led to just the book they said they would lead to. I sat on the floor in the stacks, pulling out book after book, sorting through what to cart home. Afterward, we went to Baskin-Robbins next door and I got chocolate chip mint ice cream in a bowl and my mom got a sugar cone of Rocky Road. As I watched my mom tilt her head back for the tip of that cone, chocolate running down her wrist, I started to think of her as a separate person, someone who was once a growing girl in libraries.

I decided early in life that roads lead to both excitement and home. Roads took my dad away on travels and they brought him to our driveway again, his tired arms open to us at the front door. Roads were strands through this square of land I knew, and all the world could be contained within their leadings.

Near the end of high school I was beginning to understand that the roads reaching from my house never ended; they always connected with distance and would one day separate me from my family. I felt the first fear of leaving and the first desire to go. I remember sitting on the basement sofa that year with a prayerful older friend of mine from work, telling her how scared I was about graduating from college in a few years and not knowing what to do with my life.

"I think you'll get married right out of college," she said with confidence. "You'll have a new home. You'll go right from your parents to your husband."

I held onto those words at the time, though they didn't sound as true as I wanted them to be. Besides, not having a husband was not the root of my fear. I wanted my friend to say that she knew—that God had told her—that when I graduated from college I would be safe and peaceful and make all the right decisions. Roads were becoming cold, mysterious, as I began the lifelong missing of that patch of land we cannot always know. As childhood streets shatter out in my memory, becoming wider and stranger, I remember, too, their rhythm: *You cannot stay here. Your safety is no longer safe.*

As I left those roads I heard many words from others about trusting God down unknown paths, words about how God keeps us peaceful even when all we know is war. Still I was not at peace.

Today my patch of land unravels no matter how I try to imagine the edges are secure. I live in a new place, on ancient earth, driving back and forth to work over Colorado concrete, these flattened intrusions into the wilderness. I am a part of all that is taking the land and the animals and burrowing into the hills as if the mountains will rise higher and still keep us warm. Beauty itself feels precarious, like the longing it stirs.

Some mornings during church services I feel myself sinking backward into a dark sky, anxious about the week ahead, the unknown we give ourselves to. I hold my husband's hand, let him anchor me. And the peace that comes in the midst of fear is greater than the peace I first knew, deeper than the peace of tree-lined streets and someone waiting at home. This is a peace that comes from being pushed, from continuing to drive when I can't remember where the roads go. Restlessness comes as well, both from fear and from longing, from a desire to be safe someday. And the mountains themselves come from a groaning that the earth did not ask for.

❦

When my sister, Dorie, and I were in elementary school, my dad often read to us in the evenings from The Chronicles of Narnia, or The Lord of the Rings, or Patricia St. John. In the kitchen, while we sat at the counter eating

Cheerios, or while we lay on a blanket on the floor between the refrigerator and the stove, or in our bedroom, each girl leaning against him until Dorie faded into older years of homework and reading of her own, leaving me and my dad to turn to mysteries and adventure stories: Encyclopedia Brown, *The Magic Bicycle, A Wrinkle in Time,* the Hardy Boys. Peace was not the stories, or the closed shades, or the nest of a bed, but my dad's face as he read. His eyebrows would come together at the intense parts, his mouth forming an O of dialogue, his eyes widening. I saw him read as I closed my eyes, felt the crispness of the pages as he turned them. Now, when I call him in the evening from this new season, weary from work and who I am, when I hear him listen and offer gentle thoughts from the day, I remember the stories he read at bedtime, the safety of his voice between words.

We look all our lives for an evening childhood peace, the return to it or the beginnings of it. We search for a peace that fills this present moment, and then the next. The peace that is not an emotion, the peace of knowing that our minds and bodies are purposeful in this time. We wait for the time when it will be enough to know that God is good.

Several years ago I flew from Illinois to Colorado to interview for the job I presently have. I had an evening flight back and the plane cabin glowed orange from the inside lights. The man sitting next to me, probably in his fifties, started a conversation. As we began to talk, I saw that he seemed alert at the beginning of a sentence and like a child—simple, giggly—at the end. He came across as an eight-year-old college professor.

This man told me that he lived in downtown Chicago, but he didn't get out much anymore because he couldn't drive. He paused. He had MS, he said kindly. It was diagnosed recently. His eyes were warm and wise, trying to speak louder than his awkward words and phrasing.

He told me how he had to quit his job because the disease was worsening. I asked him what he did. He smiled. "I was a brain surgeon."

He nodded at the irony. "Yes, but I can't help my own mind. All you know doesn't always make you better." We were nearing the end of the flight. We chatted more, his face going in and out of my vision as doctor, as child. As we stood to get off the plane, he helped me get my bag down from the overhead bin. My mind began shifting to my upcoming decision, my walk back to a home that might not be my home for long. "God bless you," the man said, handing me my bag. He looked straight at me. *Peace be with you.*

For a moment peace was clearer than any decision I would need to make, a peace offered from someone who had felt it sharpen in hours that brought no answer. This man knew how little we ever understand. He knew the true roads, the roads that lead us, settled, into a bold and reckless future. The nameless roads with curves that are not curves but feel frightening when you first learn to drive them.

One childhood evening, when I was just old enough to buy things with my own money, I bought a picture of Jesus at Woolworth's in West Towne Mall. A few years earlier, Emily and I had bought matching hamsters, Franklin and

Roosevelt, at the same Woolworth's. (Soon after our purchase we discovered that Roosevelt—mine—was a girl, or suspected of being a girl, and she became Rosie, just to be safe.) I thought about this as I wandered that evening, close enough to my mom to know where she was but far enough away to be shopping "alone." The pet department didn't draw me as it once had, but I stopped in front of a display of Jesus pictures. He sat, five deep, white-faced, brown-bearded, on a rock against a purple background. He was looking away, with a slight smile, His robe bright against the night around Him, a purple sash draped over His shoulder. Glue bubbled up between the cardboard backing and the picture. The image sat in a black plastic frame.

Standing in Woolworth's that evening, I realized I was scared. I realized I wanted to know that Jesus sat by me as I slept. In that cheap, Americanized, plastic picture of Christ I saw Someone watching me, always, and though I had recognized Jesus' presence with me before, I needed a reminder. *Peace be with you.*

Later I will call for my dad in the night and he will bring me a cup of water. *Just a sip.* It tastes like no other water; it is middle-of-the-night-fear water. *Close your eyes.* He seems ruffled, tired, slightly unsure of himself. *No, Mommy's asleep.* I think I hear someone outside my window. I feel the hours of unknowing, when the house and everything in me is silent and mysterious. I think of stories before bed, breakfasts, the purple Jesus picture next to me. The fear does not leave, but the peace comes. It is enough, as the door shuts behind him. I close my eyes, let rest choose me, let it carry me to morning.

Several years ago my mother was diagnosed with a malignant tumor. We waited weeks for surgery, my bones cold inside me at the thought of her dying. This was the culmination of fears—the reason, I told myself, why peace was too weak to last.

One morning soon after the diagnosis, I went back to my grad school apartment after church, collapsed on my bed, and cried for hours. When I was finally silent, my body feeling the exhaustion of spending all the tears it had, I felt the breeze of the voice of God. In His silent words there was not answer or hope. Instead, in a core of stillness, I heard God say, *I hate cancer, too.* I was not alone in wanting afternoons of grief to end. At the height of my fear I felt a strange and woody peace.

The day of my mom's surgery, we waited a swelling wait. When my dad called saying the doctors had found the tumor to be benign—saying my mother never looked so beautiful—I stood in the kitchen feeling how the call could have been different, feeling myself breathe air I had not breathed for many tight days. When I first saw her, she was coming out of the anesthesia. She took my hand, comforting. The mother.

I was tender toward what God was going to do next, toward whether the fear had lived in me long enough to take hold. We had run to the brink and been allowed to walk back. We were sipping the water we'd cried for but still waiting for morning to come.

I was reading in my mom's hospital room one afternoon during her recovery when a family friend stopped by. Not wanting to wake my mom, Paulette pulled up a chair and sat at the end of the bed. I read while Paulette watched my mom. After a half hour Paulette stood up, smiled at me, and left.

No words for me or my mom, no promises, but her silence said, *Peace be with you.* I felt the tears in my body, the stillness of the mornings before surgery. *And also with you.* How do we stand on the edge of what we do not know, with only the love of God to hold us? *Lift up your hearts!* This is a love that offers presence, a love to sit by us while we wait. *We lift them to the Lord.* So we rise, we pray, we drink this carried water in the dark. *It is right to give God thanks and praise.* We ask for a peace we do not understand, a peace that comes when all fears push against it.

After Paulette left I sat in a new kind of quiet, and watched my mom sleep.

CHAPTER THREE

All That Might Be: Hope

When hope began in my life, it was not as complicated as it is now. It was a tattered Advent calendar taped to the side of the refrigerator every December. When my mom brought out that paper calendar and secured it at little-girl level, my sister and I knew that Christmas soon would come. Every perforated door was numbered; on the back of each door were four lines of a

Christmas carol, and on the inside, as if we were looking into a house, was an image of an old-fashioned Christmas.

Dorie and I alternated opening the door each evening. Although after several years of use many of the doors hung open on their own, the opening and reading of the next day's door was a source of enjoyment, and argument, every year. It didn't take long for us to figure out who would open December 24—*double* doors, with the first lines of "Joy to the World" on the inside of the door opposite the baby Jesus. If I opened Day 1, I would not get to open Christmas Eve. Every year I tried to work my way around this, sometimes with frustration and pleading.

That calendar offered an aliveness to me, a jealousy and a peace and a richness of anticipation, each door holding hope for the most wonderful month of the year. I stared at it as my mom cooked dinner; then in the morning I looked at each door we had already opened. I watched it during the day the same way I watched the presents under the tree, wondering if I could wait until the moment of opening came.

The final door held the greatest hope, though I could not name why. It held the hope of Advent candles on Sunday nights and my mom bringing out a hidden gift for each of us from the china cabinet after dinner. School would be out, presents would wait for us, Mom and Dad would be both more busy and more relaxed, spending entire mornings and evenings with us as if they were on vacation too. All these things I reached toward, came alive, for my expectations were new and awake.

For when we reached those double doors, hope flooded from every window where we had looked for God before. We triumphed to see a God we'd expected for so long, as if we'd never doubted God would come.

⊷✕⊶

Our house on the corner of Whitcomb and Hammersley in Madison, Wisconsin, was surrounded by retirement apartments. Mr. Kellogg was a part of my childhood years, an elderly man with an evening walk and a cane he raised in greeting. The older couple on the second floor of the retirement building next to us also intertwined with my childhood, along with their cheery waves to us when we went for late-afternoon bike rides. The bike rides themselves formed in this setting, memories of weaving in and out of apartment driveways, up and down the wheelchair ramps, watching young families pull up to visit grandparents.

On one corner of our yard was a bus stop, where our older neighbors got on and off the bus when traveling downtown. A bus stop and kind people who missed their grandchildren presented an ideal situation for two girls who wanted to make money on a summer afternoon. My dad made us a wooden stand where Dorie and I sold bread and homemade potholders along with squash and cucumbers from our garden. Our neighbors sometimes brought us gifts, whether or not they bought anything, and once one woman invited us to her home across the street where she gave us two stuffed Bucky Badgers. I remember looking around her apartment and wondering where her family was and how she came to live in such a tiny place, her years compressed into an odd smell and a crowded living room.

I saw every elderly person in those years as a grandparent, representative of my grandparents. Our neighbors lived in the kind of place where grandparents lived; they seemed pleased with my presence, as my grandparents were. So I liked them and respected them and believed that all grandparents plateau to porches and waves and baseball caps. In the winter, these "grandparents" let us slide down the hill that was next to our house but not on our property. This was the hill that sloped from the tamarac tree I could see from my bedroom, the tree that was a touch point for sledding and hide-and-seek, my view from childhood. These neighbors saw us grow up, and we loved them for it.

When estate sale signs went up in our neighborhood, it meant that someone had either moved to a nursing home or died. With other Saturday shoppers, my mom and sister and I sorted through tables of basket collections, or porcelain bells, or thimbles from around the world. Half-filled bags of flour, unopened cereal boxes—it was all for sale. Here were the remnants of life and all that would not remain. Here stood the families behind the card tables, remembering how these treasures were loved, or grieving that the basket or doll or doily held secrets that would never speak. We saw this even as we took our purchases home, believing perhaps that they would last in our lives. Believing that this scrap of memory we carried down the sidewalk could be a part of our story, now that it had left someone else's.

I also remember the times an ambulance came to the building across the street. The lights of the siren pulsated in our living room and my mom stood behind us at the window as the paramedics carried someone out on a stretcher. Would he or she be back? Was it Mr. Kellogg? Was it anyone we would know well enough to miss?

I assumed that someone's heart had stopped beating—this was one of the scenarios my parents offered. I pictured a body perfectly still, waiting for someone to start it up again. I marveled that a person who had just bought a potholder at a bus stop could be helpless enough to be carried away, her face an oval poking out from a bed of white.

Estate sales and ambulance lights sound dismal, but when they are woven into childhood along with Big Wheels and snowball fights, they are just a part of growing up. I did not see the fragile bones in all the grandparents surrounding us. I saw, though, how life could change and end, and I connected that end to me. I pictured myself old, in our same house, rocking like our neighbors rocked. I did not know to feel aches as I rocked; I did not know that memories fade. I thought about how my heart kept beating, how I never had to ask it to, how sharp it felt inside me when those lights came through our living room.

Our neighbors were in a season of observing, and I was in a season of being observed. I accepted this as something that was right as I veered for the grass when my bike was going too fast on those first rides or smiled to bundled residents walking gingerly to their cars in the snow as I rushed down that backyard sledding hill.

Mr. Kellogg and the others probably had hopes for the Fryling girls on the corner, hopes greater than expectations or needs. They hoped for us to learn to ride our bikes, to find our lost dog, to live well. They hoped for the life we were growing into and they were growing away from. I was new next to them, I was all future. We waved to one another as I dangled out into a bright and promising world, as they watched with a hope I was not yet wise enough to know.

I was too young then to name hope as the burst of living surrounding me, to see how it took the form of putting on summer pajamas and sleeping with the windows open, walking in the front door from play and smelling dinner. The aching for the yes of life, the rush to have more of it.

Even the pulse of ambulance lights in our living room spoke life to me, telling me how strong my own newness was. Some days I wanted to ride my bike farther than I was allowed to and that desire, too, was life, a hope for all that was left to discover.

I saw that hope, to be hope, is alive in every way, alive with summers and wind and also with sadnesses—bright lights at night when we should be sleeping. I carried, fresh, the yearning we are born into, the reach for a world not quite in our grasp.

━━━✦━━━

As a child, I wanted to be a tomboy, with a name like "Jo" from *Little Women*. I wanted to roll up my dress and put my hair in braids and look for snakes in the river like Laura in *Little House on the Prairie*. I wanted to insist to my mother that I wear overalls. Instead, I was a small, pink girl who feared finding a spider under her pillow at night and who only played sports with her dad in the driveway—tennis and basketball and soccer after dinner on summer evenings, attempts to hit the baseball before it hit the garage door behind me. I watched with pride whenever my dad had to jog across the street to retrieve the ball I'd just sent flying. Then as a special treat, at the end of our games, my dad would hit the baseball over the house. This dad who could do anything! I scampered to find the ball and though I tried tossing it back to him, it never even reached the rain gutter. Sometimes before going inside I ran around our house to feel the ground change shape under my feet as I leapt over my mom's gardens and turned the corner by the woodpile. I had so much life in me I could scatter it as I ran and not come back to collect it later.

When the day was not good for running, my sister and I played for hours with our dollhouses, coming alive in Old West make-believe where Dorie was Mary Ingalls and I was Laura, and the story was so real I picture it now more clearly than the tiny rooms our dolls hopped through. In those houses I could be a tomboy running or a mother scolding or a father coming in from the fields, and every character, no matter his age, was clean with the hope of what his story might be.

Then on special afternoons, my mom brought out her Ginny doll for me, the doll she and her sister had played with in another time. Sitting at the dining room table, I immersed myself in thought and doll accessories—the blue, corduroy winter coat and hat, the raincoat, the paisley play outfit, the shimmering dinner gown, the tiny pearl necklace and the dangly earrings that never stayed on.

I dressed and undressed and dressed again this fragile toy with the wide-eyed stare, picturing my grandma bringing the doll out for my mom. I imagined my mom's little-girl fingers buttoning these buttons, feeling these fabrics, making the grand decision of which hat Ginny should wear to church. We were both little girls and both mothers, and we felt and knew and dreamed the same things, as we smoothed the dresses and fitted the shoes on that doll with such tenderness that she might have been eternal.

On these quiet days I felt myself running the fastest, faster than the wind outside would allow, and the memory of those hours stirs an aliveness in me still. For just as the love my mom practiced on dolls would swell into the love she had for me, the little-girl wishes that fit into a doll suitcase are still my wishes, delicacy and awe reserved for children yet to be.

Now when it rains, or nears dinnertime in the fall, I long for the coming-home hours and staying-home evenings of childhood. More, I long for my own dinner table, set for faceless children who bound down the stairs in my mind, as if I can remember what has not yet happened, miss someone not yet begun. This, too, is hope, this lingering in the past until our imaginings take shape and offer a life at last to hold.

Just before I entered high school, years after Mr. Kellogg and my early-childhood neighbors had left us in an unnoticed night, my family traveled to Vancouver, British Columbia. There my dad took a month-long class at a university, and we stayed at some friends' house while they were away. During those weeks, we bought cookie dough in large tubs from the grocery store and made cookies every day. We watched for the neighborhood cat and followed an ancient sundial around the hours. My sister and I ran ice cubes up and down each other's arms and legs when it was too hot to do much else. Some nights were so warm that my mom pulled our mattresses into the back room, and we slept on the floor with the breeze coming through the wide patio doors.

My mom made her way through the hymnbook that month, bringing chords from the piano that seemed to remind her of another time, a time before us. I wiggled one of my final baby teeth out of its home, a scary process because I hated anything that reminded me of the dentist. We went to the beach and the mountains and walked across the Capilano Suspension Bridge one weekend, teetering between where we came from and where we wanted to be and telling each other not to look down.

On several mornings in Vancouver, I padded downstairs in my pink South Dakota nightshirt and joined my dad at the breakfast table by the broad window. My mom and sister were sleeping, much to my delight, as my dad and I ate cereal and watched the sunrise before he left for class and I went back to bed. In our sleepiness, with a window to stare out, I was more willing to be with him than I would be for the next several years of adolescence.

When we returned home after our month away, I entered a storm of change. The neighbors who had taken Mr. Kellogg's place could not appreciate how hard-earned my bike rides around the block had come. Yet this was a time when the world was hopeful for me, when strangers in church or teachers in the hallway gave mini-talks on the opportunities unfolding in my life. This was also the time when disappointments crowded in on each other, not large losses or one event of disillusionment, but the daily failures that come with high school, the ongoing dissatisfaction with friendships and myself.

I remember coming home one school day furious with a friend. "I hate her, I hate her, I hate her!" I told my mom, as we sat on her bed. I was jealous of my friend's grades and looks and popularity, unsatisfied with her friendship, and annoyed that neither God nor my mom could fix it. I felt dull with life. I was far from the yelp of hope in my face that had awakened me on bike rides a few years before.

Again, I retreated to pockets of being alone, now more desperately searching the Bible for some nugget of promise. I took comfort in discovering that hope and waiting mean the same thing in some languages. With teenage angst and a spiritual hunger, I loved the book of Lamentations, its drama and longing: "My soul is downcast within me. Yet this I call to mind and therefore I have hope: Because of the LORD's great love we are not consumed. . . . " *Therefore, I will wait.* And waiting could be active, expectant, waiting could be alive.

It was several years later that I returned to Vancouver on my own and thought back on those shy breakfasts with my dad on the edge of the storm of high school. It was the summer before my last semester of graduate school, the summer before I would begin a career, the summer I swung between two worlds and felt the air rock beneath me. I was auditing two classes in the mornings, writing down my dreams in the middle of the night for fun, and trying to stay out of the heat of the sun in the afternoons.

One of my few links to people during that time was Kathryn, a red-headed young woman from Nova Scotia who was staying on the same floor as I was in the near-empty dorm. We walked to the bus together and chatted while brushing our teeth before bed. Kathryn grew up in an Irish Catholic family, the second youngest of fifteen kids. "My mom baked five loaves of bread every day," she told me one morning as we waited for the bus to come. Later, I went back to the dorm and thought about fifteen kids and five loaves of bread a day as the sun seemed to follow me, slanting onto my bed as I waited for the cooler evening to come.

On many days after class in Vancouver, I got on a bus going downtown and rode until I was tired of riding. I bought lunch at a deli, wove in and out of used book-stores, watched students steer their bikes or knapsacks or cellos onto the seat in front of me. I was hopeful about the changes waiting for me when I returned to Chicago, yet hopes I didn't know I had, fell one after another.

Marriage. Deeper friendships. Clarity about the future. A career I loved. Peace. I prayed and read and took long notes in class and no revelation about God came. Each day I tried to hold what I knew of God and gather faith, in pieces, around me as I listened. *I can be expectant because of who I believe God is. Hope is more than these things I dream about, it is living out the story as it comes.*

During those weeks of classes and silence, I began to take again the frightening lightness of waiting for the next moment of life to begin. And hope can grow on its own, this silent God-gift, in buses and dorm rooms, the sun hot and piercing on long and patient afternoons.

⟞⟝

A few years ago, my friend Kirsten and I attended a conference in Michigan. A good conference, with good people, but I was tired, weary from travel and long hours of work and the unfamiliar days of early marriage. I felt worn out, a baby working every day to grow. The future was finally with me and yet it seemed too much to think about. The "hopes and fears of all the years" pressed in.

On our second evening at the conference, we enjoyed dinner with an author and her agent, and afterward the two of us drove back to our motel in our rental car. A mix CD blared Van Morrison and Sting through the stereo as we passed through the cobble-stoned streets of old Grand Rapids, the convertible top down, and I felt myself awaken. I felt the heat from the car too warm on my legs, the April air too cold on my face, and I wanted it hotter and colder still. I wanted the wind to sting my eyes, the night too dark to see, the street lights too bright to stand under. I wanted to risk hope, yell it out like I used to when I believed it was true.

It's going to be OK, the cold and heat and dark seemed to say. Waiting and hope could redeem one another. I felt I could not take in another sensation—how could I be more weary? How could I hold more fear?—and yet I wanted my soul to stir more, to wake me and remind me of all I'd forgotten in the darkness of fatigue.

Yes, this is what it feels like to be very hot, very cold, very thirsty, very angry, very alive. I could get out of this car and run, I could soar down streets on my bike, God and I together. Hope was far beyond me, more powerful than I could imagine. Hope would come where it didn't belong, it would press out tears like wine. It would come wrapped in thankfulness or loneliness, careening into a prayer or a car ride, calling out its name.

CHAPTER FOUR

Between the Mysteries:

Wonder

I am in the back seat of our station wagon next to my mom, driving to visit grandparents. I am loved. I see color, Christmas lights out the window, and I want to be close to them. I reach as they pass by.

From this first memory I make wide leaps through dreams, floating through the years of the very young. The lights separate themselves to the red apple on the back porch and the yellow wallpaper by my crib and the aqua carpet we danced on before bed. And I am stirring, waking, as I live as children live, gulp color like sugar, and remember the beat between the mystery and the reaching.

———◆———

As my mom and I walked to the car after my kindergarten screening, the leaves and sidewalk and sun were bright around me.

"Why did you tell Miss Halverson you could only count to ten?" my mom asked.

I shrugged. I wasn't used to strangers asking me questions about what I knew and didn't know. It seemed personal and unnecessary.

"Did you not like talking to her?"

I shrugged again. *That was all I wanted to show her. She doesn't even know me.* My mom had waited in the other room while the teacher pried at my knowledge. My reward at the end of my interview was a cookie, which I ate while Miss Halverson and my mom talked in the "mouse house" part of the classroom.

Ten was a lot of numbers just by themselves, I believed. Enough to think about for a good length of time. *1,* the proud, bold number in the left corner of my mind. *2,* weak but gentle; *3,* cocky but alone; *4,* strong and kind; *5,* the mothery older sister; *6,* shy, dependent on *4; 7* was quiet and not that smart; *8* was smart and knew it; *9,* the brother watching from near the top; and *10,* the grandfather, wise and strong in the upper right of my head. So quickly we could say these, show them off, without thinking about each one, without lingering to consider all they knew and would not tell us. But Miss Halverson did not ask me about this.

"You can count to one hundred, can't you?" my mom asked as we got into the car.

I nodded. As we drove home, I was unaware that I was on the brink of many years of questions and invasions, discoveries and rewards. It was in kindergarten that my universe of numbers and letters would begin to expand. Numbers soon had to curve to the right in my head because I had not allowed enough space for them to grow straight up past 100. The alphabet, beginning with that pink leader of an *A*, coursing through the parental *M* and *N*, rushing to the browns and blacks of *X*, *Y*, *Z*, formed itself in a different part of my mind, unfolding bright and hopeful, left to right like the line of letters across a chalkboard. Days of the week formed a tight blue circle; the year a broader, yellow circle, enough to hold a birthday and a Christmas and the summer vacation that the years would come to pivot on.

In kindergarten we sat on the floor by Miss Halverson's rocking chair repeating these things, spelling our names, saying our addresses and telephone numbers and what to do if we got lost. I sorted through the fact that I was given so much more to hold in my mind—the lives of letters and numbers and dates now awakened and restless—and no one around me seemed to think this was remarkable, and tiring, and new.

The rush of life peaked when I learned that letters were not just stories on their own; they formed stories when put together. The first book I read was about an apple tree; every time the word *apple* would have appeared, a picture of an apple appeared instead. The book was six or eight pages, on thin, shiny paper, and Miss Halverson let me take it home one night to show my parents. I read it to my dad that evening in our blue recliner. The thrill of walking around the room that adults knew, of telling my dad a story just as he told stories to me—all mystery, all poetry held between my hands in a wrinkled paper book.

I was applauded for reading, but I wanted the words themselves to be applauded, too. A celebration was in order, I believed, for the fact that books and apples existed at all. Wonder, that tenacious birth, flailed in a cold world it did not want to enter.

When I learned of numbers that reached higher than I could see, I tried to imagine counting, counting, never coming to an end. Not every number could have a personality, I realized. Except for the occasional attention-getter—*777, 150, 1000*—after 100 they started to take on the characteristics of each other. I began to stretch as well, leaving behind what could have been thought about for such a long time, the place where the unseen begins.

❧

My teachers were weary in those early years and though they were often kind, they did not see me. They moved us through alphabets and recesses and told us how to write our names in the right place on our math worksheets and did not look for mystery in-between the letters and the numbers floating towards us.

By the time I reached third grade, books were passing through my hands at a steady pace—Beverly Cleary, a child's biography of Harriet Tubman, various horse stories. Third grade was the year a wondrous teacher came to me like a fairy godmother, a twinkle to her as if she wanted to tell us she was from our own land but she needed to wait until the outsiders left. A college football fan, Mrs. Pearl wore red and white on game days and sometimes led us in a chorus of "On Wisconsin" before class. She let us choose our own spelling words, let us color while she read to us in the afternoon, and assigned me the first journal I ever kept. My most vivid memory of Mrs. Pearl is when she called us to the window to see the first snow of the season. She was as excited as we were. I looked out on the playground that day and the snow seemed white and bizarre, just because Mrs. Pearl thought it was. She had created a space for the astonishing to arrive.

In third grade, my thoughts felt a freedom to enjoy themselves and I looked forward to school, feeling giggly about it when I got ready for bed at night. Whether Mrs. Pearl believed in God or not, I don't know. But looking back I see that she did believe in mystery, she did believe in wondering. Like most children given the freedom to imagine, one of the things I wondered about was God.

It had been several years since wonder had led me to "ask Jesus into my heart" as I sat in my room alone, walking my feet up the bedroom wall and back down again. I had imagined Jesus knocking on a wooden door inside me (the same door I would later picture as Bilbo Baggins's in *The*

Hobbit) as if he had been there before but needed an invitation to return. On many nights since then, I had asked him in again, sometimes ten or twelve times before I went to sleep, just to make sure he had understood my call. But it was in third grade that I realized how many thoughts I could think of God before bed, and how deeply buried they could be. God could not be explained and this did not bother me. I could not explain snow or story or color either but still they appeared.

Third grade was my last year to be in the same class as my best friend Emily, the year before friendships evolved to a language I did not know how to speak. It was the year before I had a sharp teacher who did not want to know my secrets, the year before all giggles seemed directed to me. Make-believe in any form would become dangerous, too risky to admit to others. So from Mrs. Pearl's world of books and safety I would tuck away the delight of imagining God imagining me, the joy of knowing I was once dreamed up. I was a mystery too, not to be explained. I was a story being told.

⬛×⬛

One summer in Madison soon after my Mrs. Pearl year, rain did not come. My sister and I worried about the faceless farmers we heard about on the news and wondered if their horses would have enough to eat. My mom taught us how to crack eggs on the sidewalk to see if they would fry and got out a bucket of snow for each of us that she had saved in the freezer from last winter. We ran our pinwheels around the yard and complained about the heat and watched the sky for the cozy blackness that would shoo us inside.

It was the middle of the night when rain arrived that summer, and Dorie and I were so thrilled for ourselves and farmers everywhere that we raced to the living room windows in our nightgowns to watch the storm come in. Thunder rolled towards us like answered prayer, water cleaning us with sound because we had trusted it would come. Faith and wonder together pressed in, hands to a window, as the trees that were strong just that afternoon bowed near to our faces in the green winds.

We hauled that storm in as long as we could, our parents still sleeping, before we scurried back to bed, confident that crops were ripening as we slept. All droughts would end that night, we believed, just as we believed that the water in arms and lakes and jellyfish was the same water hurrying from the sky. No mystery was too much to consider.

It was years later when I was an adult that another drought came to my summer, this time in Colorado dryness. There was no time for pinwheels that year, little room for looking to the sky except at traffic lights that stretched too long. I was tired at night, not from all I did not understand but from all I did understand, not from the newness of an alphabet but from keeping up with the familiar. Books themselves, my early doors into wonder, were plentiful and messy in my editor's office. Letters lined up lost their marvel as I crunched them to fit a page.

And the sky turned off. We counted again and again the days it did not rain. Pine trees browned, grass fell brittle to the wind. Nearby forest fires blew ash on our cars, sunsets turned an eerie gold, smoke filled our throats. We were a desert, a rage, a piece of ground.

July Fourth fireworks were canceled—too dangerous— park fountains fizzled, sprinklers were regulated. Water was golden. All we had was all we were going to get. We tsked at the sunburned ground and drank more fully than before. This novelty, this jewel. I remembered how I used to play with water as a child, feel it light and heavy across my fingers. I had not stared at water in so long.

Rain came that year, not in a grand storm but in brief afternoon showers, and then winter arrived and the mountains opened wide to catch and store the snow for us. Water would retreat to the ordinary until next summer.

As a little girl I was amazed not only at the storm outside my window but at the rain I believed would come one day. The expectation itself was marvelous to me. *Reach for the sky,* my mom used to tell us when she pulled our little-girl shirts off before bed. *So high!* Maybe the water that fell on me that Colorado summer was the same water that bubbled on our driveway the morning after our storm in Madison. Maybe some things are worth imagining.

<hr />

We went to church nearly every Sunday during my childhood, often rushed and cranky as we fell into the car. When we returned home, my mom got the popcorn started and my dad made grilled cheese sandwiches. We all changed clothes and sat down for lunch in our places, with our sandwiches made and cut to preference, and sighed ourselves into a Sunday afternoon. The day was alive, brief, scrubbed clean.

On some Sunday afternoons when I was finished with my grilled cheese and was done making tornadoes with the grease on my plate, I would pluck a popcorn kernel from the jar in the kitchen, take a Styrofoam cup from the pantry, gather some dirt from the soil bag in the garage, and plant what I was sure would become a stalk of corn.

My mom had a planter in her bedroom, a three-tiered planter with white gravel and fluorescent bulbs. Green pots of African violets sat on the shelves, just as they sat on my grandfather's shelves in Iowa. My mother learned a love of gardening from her father. He still sends her an amaryllis bulb every year at Christmas, ordered from a catalog delivered to his nursing home, and calls to make sure she is caring for it correctly. This deep red bulb, this purity of beginning again.

I did not find my mom's violets pretty, but I liked watching her care for them, I liked how they were hers. And on certain Sunday afternoons, I shimmied the Styrofoam cup into the gravel in that planter. Over the next week I watered it when my mom watered her violets, watched the puddle round and fall in the soil. Soon a green sprout appeared, so willing to bring its tall promise into such a tiny realm. I watched it grow, perfect, watched it reach to the top of the violet planter.

I sometimes tried planting my cornstalk outside, but it never lived past that first perfect bursting. So my mom's violets lived on alone in their planter, velvety and rich, and I marveled at the secret I had: an Orville Redenbacher popcorn jar held life.

Now I watch my husband garden, my favorite kind of watching to see him intent on planting, weeding, watering. He enjoys these plants as his mother does and I think of the unseen threads we take up from those who love us. He and I both watch roses struggle to bloom in a foreign climate, hens-and-chickens scatter among their rocks. We watch, too, each other, surprised that we are here in this marriage, this season of marvel.

Such mysteries we hold, as if we could stare at them long enough to understand. We reach while keeping close to what we know. And I sit in desert air sipping water, watching deep red bulbs of memory bury themselves inside me, waiting for a burst of green to come to a world too small to contain it.

CHAPTER FIVE

Pieces of Ourselves:
Relationship

Emily with yellow braids was there as I emerged into awareness of life. We met somewhere between kindergarten and first grade, her friendship folding into my consciousness as if she had been waiting all along for me to walk out of the gray syllables of preschool and into the effort of relational language. Before I knew to choose her, we were picking berries from the bushes in my backyard, rushing through the patio door with double handfuls of purple, plunking the berry-knots into a mixing bowl on the kitchen counter and running back out for more. Sticky and blue and happy, we stirred our berries into paste with no purpose beyond the sound of berry juice squishing against the side of the bowl, slurping to the countertop.

During recesses in elementary school, we played in our secret fort in the woods behind the playground—the tree with stairstep roots and the leafy alcove between its trunks. The yelps of the schoolyard faded as we made a kitchen and a bedroom, a deck and a front porch, all from a circle of space that let us twirl inside it. One of us was the child and the other the mother, and then we switched, eating and drinking the airy food and drink of little girls. I'd make my hands a pillow and sleep the deep hours of make-believe, feel the woods rustle beside me, the ground alive under my head.

Our arguments, those hot and vicious fights, withered in a day or two, bleeding into an unquestioning loyalty as we watched ourselves materialize into individuals who had relationships outside of our families. Emily didn't laugh at me when I got glasses in third grade, and she was the one to be quiet with me when I learned my hamster, Rosie, had died. She offered the height of friendship by promising without words that I would always have someone to sit with at lunch, and that if I wanted to save her a seat on the first day of school, she would take it.

During the school year, we watched *He-man* on weekdays at 3:30 before pretending we were the Wonder Twins. And on summer days, when the school was ghostly and alone, we curled like commas in the cool metal of the playground barrel, believing that here in this rounded cement of a home, perhaps everything could be safe.

⁂

Does everything seem smaller looking back? Even the books I loved once can grow tighter when I read them again, the wide room they once brought me to, ordinary and boxed. And I see now that the space waiting beside Emily that seemed so grand and complete was narrow after all. In memory, our house in the woods was just a tree, with branches the junior high boys would climb at dusk, and our conversations had the limits we set for them. Emily barely mentioned that her parents were getting divorced. All my questions seemed wrong. The hiding places we used to have with each other separated to their own confines, our words darting out and retreating again on recess walks until we heard the whistle call us inside.

At the end of our fifth-grade year, Emily and I were playing video games in an outdoor arcade at a water park birthday party when she told me she was moving forty-five minutes away to Sun Prairie. I remember the cement felt wet and grainy under my feet, and the sun was behind her when she went back to the slides, and I lingered in the arcade until it was time to go home.

Later I would visit her at her mom's new house and feel awkward. Our friendship was suddenly tiny, and she was letting me go on without her. We sat on the bed in her new bedroom and the room was just a room, the window looking out to ordinary trees you might not even notice. We were leaving to discover others who had not shared our imaginary drink; we were far from those first moments of recess when we raced to the woods, time waiting for us as if it always would.

—⨯—

As my uncle and I drive to his house from the airport, I tell him about Emmanuelle, a girl I met in France when I was in high school. I always meant to keep in touch with her but we never wrote.

"I tell you, Elisa, that happens again and again in life," my uncle says. I see how his mouth looks like my dad's. I have never noticed this before, even in all those years of Christmases and vacations together. I want to stare at the way his lips round themselves as he talks, forming words as if telling me bedtime stories. "I wish I had kept up with more of my relationships, but now they're gone. God puts people in our lives for a reason. When we let them go, we are letting go of what is most precious."

My uncle retired a few years ago and he and my aunt moved home from Hong Kong. It is unsettling to me that his life is full of friends, children, grandchildren, but still he regrets the people he has lost. *But it's been so busy, we have so many people now whom we could love,* I want to say, wanting my suspicions to not be true.

Is losing friendship less than a kind of death? We use phrases like "became friends," "broke up," "lost touch," "built a relationship," because we try to name what cannot be named, to square in the mystery. Just as we mention the roof of a home, the color of walls, the age of the wood in the floors, we refer to a relationship in parts and time frames as if it did not, after all, house us completely, steady and warm and cover us since before we could choose to let it.

One evening when I was living alone I came home from work and found a drawer open, just as it was when I left. It struck me that I could be gone for hours or months and my apartment would look the same when I returned, untouched by another's movement. Trapped in the spaciousness of my days, I wanted to scream out my need for people, my longing not to grow dusty.

It's in unexpected moments that I realize how much I want someone who knows the coffee I like, knows how I feel about my parents looking older, how I've been sleeping and what book I would like to read next. I need others to keep my thoughts out of the grooves they can stay in on their own.

Though at times relationship seems too rickety a shelter to enter, pummeled by change and teased by our weaknesses, the desire to know others remains. If God lets that longing cling as it does, that desperate quiet for companionship, perhaps it's worth understanding, perhaps later we will turn to the buildings we once thought were so thin and see them as fortresses that held us, frail and failing though we were at the time.

Now that I know the space of my need for others and how it hungers to be filled, I feel a greater shyness for relationships I assumed would last, and a shyness for their ending. I am hesitant to think of Emily, not because we were friends and then were not, but because in all those years of lunch hours I did not question her, God, myself, or anyone who might upset the balance that I did not know was precarious.

When you're five, or eight, on the tire swing, or finding your locker on the first day of school, no one tells you that friendships will be a part of you. The giggles and games and sleepovers, the turned backs and whispers and sassy words. They are coloring you in, creating you, excavating you, bringing you to life again and again, these birth-deaths of relationships.

⋈

Perhaps people are prone to diminish when we turn to remember them because they, in unnamed stretchings, are prone to expand us. How could the soul not grow in knowing that a room exists that will comfort you, hold your secrets in its corners, that one person will save a place for you at the table and look for you to arrive there?

I'll never again see my husband for the first time open the door with a mug of tea in his hand, our second date. But this loss made room for me to know more of him, allowed us to move in the space God leaves between us. For though we clamber to be closer to each other, God never lets us know what it is like to live another's life. Very nearly we get to the abyss that keeps us from another's soul, but even there God will have us reach across an absolute separation, feel our own soul grow as it moves unceasing toward another.

I learn more and more about Eric, but I do not understand how his thoughts travel, what tiny moment formed him in his childhood, what he feels, in all its essence, toward me. And he doesn't know what it is like for me to miss him, what throaty emotion comes when I think of him and he is not there. A scent, a nuance, a wave of unnamedness that is more real than hearing him walk through the door. These are the secrets God has us keep as we expand ourselves for each other.

When I was in eighth grade, my mom asked a family friend of ours if she might be willing to get together with me occasionally to talk. So Mary and I started meeting every Saturday morning at Big Boy, then Lane's Bakery, then Sundance Café. We met for breakfast once a week for five years, and over pancakes Mary and I formed a friendship with room to change. We read books together, we talked about what didn't make sense in the Bible, I complained about the confusion of being a teenager, and Mary affirmed the murkiness of adolescence. The stories Mary told me about her marriage, her pregnancies, her children, were the first I would hear of such things from someone outside our family. Today I pull out her words often to look at them, as I now live the season of life she lived in front of me.

During this time, I started baby-sitting for Mary's daughter, Abigail, who was born when I was thirteen. Mary or her husband, David, would pull up in a red station wagon at 5:30 every Saturday night and, as we drove to their house, we talked about my classes and David and

Mary's work and Abigail. Some weeks, David helped me with science and calculus before I baby-sat, my notes and textbooks spread out over the desk in his home office.

Now when I visit with Mary over breakfast, I sense that we are not having this breakfast only, we are having the past fifteen years of breakfasts. We are speaking words that have been rising to an audible volume since we first met and listening with an understanding that began in an unremembered moment. I feel time spill over into the companionship of this conversation.

⁂

David and Mary hosted a wedding shower for me at their home several years ago, my first trip back to Madison since the year my parents had moved. The cold came in the door with every person, along with a gush of stories of relationship. My childhood Sunday school teacher, girls I had baby-sat for, my former youth group leader, two high school friends, my first boss.

Jane Brown, my childhood next-door neighbor, came in with her cane and hugs and "Oh, honey!" Jane's husband, Harry, had died when I was very young. We had seen cars pulled up at her house late into the evening and my mom had gone over to check on her. "Never stop telling each other you love each other," Jane tells Eric and me at the shower. "And don't stop touching—hold hands, touch each other's arm, give each other hugs." I nod and take this in because the kind of love she has known must be listened to.

Later, David takes pictures and the kids run around the fireplace and I introduce Eric to people and listen as others tell him stories about me. I watch the faces of friends who have known great sorrow since I've seen them last, hear how their words sound thicker and stronger. And I bring a newness home to what is familiar as the evening, and the years, and the goodness, begin to overflow.

I find Emily on the Internet, an undramatic ten-minute search. Right age, right location, right last name. After sending an e-mail, I tell Eric that even if it is the right Emily, she may not write back because she might think I'm intrusive. After all, I tell him, she didn't sit by me at the last spelling bee of elementary school, and I wanted to spend too much time together the summer before she moved. Eric nods. "I think she's probably gotten over that by now."

Emily writes back, the right Emily, and over e-mail we fill each other in on the last seventeen years, important things to know like college, marriage, jobs, our parents and sisters. But what I want to ask is what she is doing this evening, if she shops at Target, if she likes to listen to Nanci Griffith. What bridge of moments brought her to this moment.

We exchange phone numbers and I wait several days to call her. How do little girls ever choose each other? I do not remember where we met, what her voice used to sound like, what she looked like when she laughed, what kind of clothes she wore. I remember a few sentences we spoke to each other, jingling around like remnants I have from the beginning of a journey—not necessarily treasures in themselves, but valuable because they are what I have kept.

When I finally call, we talk for half an hour, jumping through time from high school to college to career. Her voice sounds the same, now that I hear it, as we chat about other elementary-school friends whom we vaguely recall. I wonder what she thinks about God. I wonder what great or small things she has lost since I last saw her.

We say good-bye with words about getting together sometime, both pleased to meet again and perhaps relieved the conversation is drawing to a close. We know each other now, and though we may not keep up the knowing, we have taken the energy to begin again, as if to redeem the loss.

I feel too defenseless to ask her if she remembers the fort or the berries or the arcade. What if I lived our friendship more than she did? But we each lived it through our own imaginations, the only way we know to live, and however small it seems now does not diminish the power it once had. The tree is just a tree but what else could it be? Why should it remain the same though we ourselves change?

⬥⟩⟨⬥

My most vivid memory of learning to play the violin in fourth grade is looking out the window, though I rarely took my eyes off the teacher. It was my mind that drifted out into the schoolyard, to the middleschoolers plodding in late for class and the thirdgraders shrieking at recess. When Nicole Conners got caught staring outside, her punishment was to write an essay on what she saw. This sounded appealing to me, but I never found the nerve to get caught. Instead I slouched next to Christine, the best student in the class, and tried not to swat the stand with my bow while we waited for Mr. Weaver to finish talking to the cello section.

Every year our class prepared for the Strings Festival, a city-wide concert of about fifteen songs ranging from easy to difficult. We could only play songs at the concert that we had "passed" by memorizing them and playing them back for our teacher in the weeks before the festival.

Through late-elementary school and early-middle school, Christine rolled through the early pieces each year, then the full-page pieces, and it soon began to bother me that her fingers and bow were quicker than mine. Sometimes I wanted my own sound to fade out the window behind us.

It took me some time to realize that it wasn't Christine's fault that she played well, and she didn't seem to hold it against me either. We began to pass notes during class and to study together when we had homework. We shared rides in the morning and played computer games together after school. As I tugged my violin out every other day for orchestra, she drew hers from its case with care, gliding the rosin along the bow and tuning the strings to a sound in her head that I pried for and could never reach.

I never did make it to the end of a Strings Festival packet. My freshman year of high school I tried hard to forget my violin in the orchestra room on weekends until the day I went to our conductor's office and let him know I was switching to study hall.

Christine continued on, through performances and rehearsals and solos in our sloping auditorium. We went to

Westgate Mall together to pick out a dress for her concerto concert, we drove downtown for her performance at the Civic Center, I met her for ice cream after a concert in college. Years later, she came to visit me in Colorado and asked me if I thought I was going to marry my boyfriend, Eric, and laughed at my confidence when I said yes.

Last summer, Eric and I went to hear Christine's New York orchestra play in Vail and we arrived late, just in time to slip into our seats and look for her brown hair clipped back as it was when I sat behind her in Mr. Horris's orchestra. After the concert, the three of us got sandwiches at a basement diner and ate and talked in the space of an airy friendship. Nothing replaces the history of a relationship, the stories that we can finish for each other because of a long affection.

The next day, Eric and I meandered through the gardens by the amphitheater as we waited to meet Christine after her rehearsal. The orchestra's music coasted over to us and we sat down on rocks to listen. So many concerts I have heard Christine play and still they startle me, the beauty God lets start again each time.

After the music faded to shuffles and talking, Christine and I got lunch wraps and smoothies and wandered around town, and people stopped her to ask if she played with the orchestra and to thank her for her music.

That night, Eric and I drove home as Christine got ready for another concert. We wove through construction and Loveland Pass and though I never heard it, I imagine Christine tuned her violin as she does before every concert and waited, sitting tall, for the conductor to pull out the music from each section like threads, and weave the notes towards one another.

It was a small weekend, a trinket to remember, and life is made up of trinkets, relationships built from a collection of moments strung together. Sometimes, I look back on a concert or a friendship or a prayer and I understand: We're not meant to leave the way we came.

CHAPTER SIX

The Missing Hours:

Time and Opportunity

In third grade I decided I was tired of time. Time to get up, time to go to recess, time for dinner, time for bed. The adult world of hours and minutes seemed boring, restrictive.

So one fall weekday morning my mom offered me the gift of a timeless day. I had the day off from school and my sister didn't—a gift in itself. When I woke up I found all the clocks in the house had been covered. My mom and I drove to the country town of Waunakee where we had breakfast at O'Malley's Restaurant, sitting just the two of us under numerous decorative hens and cows. We wandered around Ben Franklin's knowing we could take as long as we wanted, went bowling at Waun-a-Bowl, got a snack at a McDonald's drive-thru, and then decided to stop at a movie theater and see what was playing. After the movie, which we only missed the first few minutes of, we drove home and tried to guess what time it was. For a day, I had felt all opportunity stretch before me. Without time, we might decide to do anything.

I tried hard to figure out, in those days, what made time exist and what existed before time. Sometimes I would close my eyes and try to feel time going past me, try to bend my thoughts to minutes I could live only once. *Catch it! Did you feel it? There it goes again.* I pictured God waiting to begin the world and get time rolling, and I wondered how He knew when to start, if He had no beginning or end. What did it look like to see hours churn on earth below, to see time ground us with limits and possibilities?

Although my grandparents' basements held things that spoke of time past, to me they offered every opportunity of the future. My Grandma Fryling kept canned soups and vegetables on the shelves leading down the basement steps, the same steps my dad once rode his tricycle down when he was three. The door at the bottom of the stairs led to the alley where my dad used to play ball and my grandma grew pansies, but more interesting to me as a child was the basement itself, full of my great-grandmother's hats and vases, old umbrellas. My grandma ironed blouses and handkerchiefs there, a multitude of hangers swinging from the pipes above her head. A small room at the back was my grandfather's old office where he kept important, masculine things like adding machines.

From a tall metal cabinet I pulled out the board games my dad played as a boy, and I carted them upstairs in search of a playmate. Scotty the doorstop-dog was in the basement, as was Agatha, the doll that I played with every year at spring break until the Easter when my grandmother packed up Agatha and all of Agatha's accessories to send home with me down the Pennsylvania turnpike. Mothballs and dust and my grandmother's whistling waft up those basement stairs in my memory and sometimes every longing I have comes back to wanting to smell that basement smell again.

My mom's parents had an overflowing basement as well, toys and games locked away in wooden cabinets under the window, puzzles in the secret compartment under the stairs. It wasn't until my grandparents prepared to move to a retirement home that I reached back deep in those cabinets. My mom and I sorted through what would not be moved while she told me stories about the house—the months her own grandmother came to stay and slept every night on the basement couch, the time my aunt caught my mom cheating at hopscotch on the cold green-and-white tile floor, how my mom sewed her wedding dress in the guest room where Dorie and I slept. We found a wooden

Monopoly game and Brownie, the stuffed dog with the missing eye that I named after my mom's childhood Welsh corgi. That afternoon a sparrow flew in the open window above us and I watched my grandpa guide it out as I held Brownie on my lap.

My grandparents would sell much of our basement-findings at a garage sale that weekend. They would be the ones behind the card tables saying good-bye. But I kept Brownie, and the stories, and held on to these things as secrets that had formed my mom, believing that I would have my own secrets one day. I was living what would become my past and this felt hopeful to me, freeing, knowing that so much of life was still left to live.

I did not understand that my mom, sifting through those childhood remnants, or my grandparents, taking the flag down in their yard and folding it in a box after forty years, might be thinking of the things that could have been and were not, might be reminiscing about how they could not go back and make different choices. I knew many kinds of time, but not the time that we regret. I knew the flattened minutes it took to eat the one spoonful of applesauce required before I could leave the table. The half-hour of piano practice that dragged out a Saturday afternoon. The evenings playing SPUD outside that blinked away as if we had put on our sneakers three minutes ago. The space alone after a fight with my parents, when time was hot and slug-gish and the house itself felt raw. And somewhere in memory I knew the ache of waking up from a nap as a toddler and being alone. No time since had ever seemed so long, those minutes before my mom appeared in the doorway. In those early days, time shaped itself to the emotion of the event. Time was its own character, complete until the next beat began.

⊷⊶

Today my grandparents look back not in days but in seasons, wide arcs that leap from world news to dinner table conversations, children born and then bringing their children home to visit. My Grandma Fryling is eighty-eight years old, and she tells me of the busyness and slowness of her days, now that most choices other than loving and praying lie behind her. The time between meals is a moment, the time from waking to pulling the bedspread off at night feels like an hour, maybe two, and yet the moments waiting for the doctor or the medicine to arrive are achingly slow, beyond any control to hurry them.

"Oh, to be eighty again," my Grandpa Watts says dryly, now in a retirement home in Iowa. My grandparents have lost many opportunities over the years, lost them to the Second World War, to illness and phone calls and late nights working at the restaurant. Lost them, too, to the strangeness of letting treasures fall from your hand so you can hold the one thing, that rough bauble of a need, that seems to be worth keeping.

⊷⊶

It was soon after I sat down for coffee with Ruth, a new friend, that she told me she thought I was driven. *Hmmmm. Do you know me enough to start out that way?* I thought. Instead I laughed lightly, in a nondriven, even spiritual kind of way, and said something about liking to work hard. Working hard is acceptable; drivenness borders on acceptable sin at best. In some ways, I was flattered that Ruth thought I was "driven." *I show that I commit to things, I appear ambitious—peaceful, but ambitious. It's working!* But Ruth's comment dangles in front of me every night I come home too late from work or lean into a choice that will satisfy for the moment but later abandon me to regret, that misplaced sorting out of memories. It chastises the spirit to sacrifice for what is not worthy of sacrifice; I feel it as a knot in my mind, the grief of investing in what will not last. And I think of all I have offered easily when the offering should have been wrenched, torn. *God, let me feel the weight of the things that are true.*

Regret itself is a sign of maturity, an ushering into the winter that we know in some part of us. I am now in between the game days of childhood and the waiting days of my grandparents and I feel the presence of every poem that gave up its chance to be written. Did those cabinets of my grandparents hold disappointment that I did not see as a girl? Did they tell of choices that could not be made again? Did they, in a quiet year, harbor a note or a hope or a scrap of memory, waiting for someone to notice and say, *Yes, this is how I want to live?*

I was in fourth grade when Halley's comet streaked by. Our teacher told us we might see it again but she never would. I had no concept then of seventy-six years, of how short and long that time span is. Many of our class assignments that year and the next centered around time travel, futuristic space homes, and what we thought life would look like in a thousand years. We also studied the Oregon Trail, a mere hundred years ago, and wrote journals as if we were pioneer children headed west. The past seemed as plausible to me as the future—both were strange, unreal. I had little concept for a reality beyond the present. Now, it is the present I fight to recognize as I tug and manipulate, stretch the canvas of an event over time that it does not span.

Several years ago the present collided with me like a shadow at my feet, and I could not shake it. The small publishing house I worked for at the time was in financial trouble—our boss told us with wry humor to lick the plastic forks after staff lunches because they were the only ones we had. The news that we had been bought out by another house thickened the afternoon with a disappointment we could not see beyond.

The next two months meant packing boxes, turning in keys, and leaping into a future that was suddenly blank. I was the only one who would move to Colorado with the new company, so files and Post-its and e-mails of the past came to my desk. I became the keeper of all that was started and not finished or finished and let go. I would be the one to see if plans took off or never got beyond a future meeting. I sank into Ecclesiastes: "So what do people get for all their hard work?"

That December I thought often of the confession, "Forgive us for all we have done and all we have left undone." *May I regret what you regret and receive what you ask me to receive.* Such a spacious prayer we can pray when we are not sure of either the path ahead or the path behind us. *Forgive us for the forgotten, forgive us for all we know and all we do not know.* The choices I'd made and would make carried the weight of eternity and yet they were wisps, nothing, in the breath of God. *Forgive us now and again, forgive us for not believing that you allow us moments of the undone.* In the timelessness of God we wait for the next minute to begin.

⸺✕⸺

When my dad was a boy, every year he and his mom and brother would go to Ocean City, New Jersey, for vacation. There my dad played Skeeball, ran on the beach with my uncle, lapped up root beer-flavored water ices. And every evening for a week my grandfather arrived on the commuter train from Philadelphia to have dinner with his family and walk with my grandma down the boardwalk. That Friday evening he would come to stay for vacation himself, and the wet salt air would be for all of them.

Dorie and I knew these stories and heard the pleasure in my dad's voice to tell them, so Ocean City became for us not only a place of vacation with Grandma and Grandpa when we were growing up, but the place of a happy childhood. We went there for a day every spring break, the boardwalk path offering such promise in its woody sounds that we nearly expected to find my dad as a ten-year-old look up from his water ice as we walked past. As we rode surrey bikes and braved the ocean with our toes, my grandparents received the day for us from a bench. I watched them smiling in our direction and tried to picture them chatting with friends, playing in the water, chasing after my dad and uncle.

The day we drove to Ocean City for the last time took the shape that only last times take. Both my grandparents were growing frail, and it would be that day at the ocean that we realized my grandpa's vision was not fading, not a tunnel closing in or a gauze sliding down, but he couldn't *see*. This was the intimacy he and my grandma were keeping, the dimness he did not talk about. How could he describe the light that came only from the left of one eye? How could he explain how long it takes to say good-bye to color?

We fell into a silence looking at our menus for lunch, aware of my grandfather staring straight ahead, and my grandparents began to laugh. "It's just that Herbie can't see, so I read him the menu," my grandma said. "But then he can't hear, so he asks me what I said, but I can't remember! You see why it takes us so long to order these days." They started laughing again, laughing because they were old and loving each other.

We finished our meal and led my grandparents to a bench, and I tried to get my mom to buy me souvenirs at the boardwalk shops. Then Dorie and I looked for shells on the beach, tugging them out of their beds and tossing them away if they were incomplete, their brokenness first buried. The top contenders to take home we carried sandy in our pockets, taking them out to compare them with each new discovery and with each other's findings, until we cushioned our best choices in our palms and wandered back to the family. "Oh, that's *nice*, honey," my grandpa said, smoothing his fingers over my collection. He seemed to know them well, understood their feel, their musty salt smell.

When it was time to go home, my dad went to get the car and the rest of us eased ourselves away from the water. As we waited at the edge of the parking lot, I inspected my shell collection, dusting sand out of the crevices, and my mom and grandmother talked. When I looked up, my grandpa had turned on the boardwalk, his face to the ocean and the seagulls. I walked up behind him but didn't know what to say to let him know I was there. I imagined the blackness in front of him, time hiding all he once loved. He wore his brown beret and carried his cane and I felt him feel every memory of Ocean City roll towards him on the waves. Then he smiled as if hearing a secret he had to tell: "Isn't it beautiful?"

CHAPTER SEVEN

Jumping In: Courage

In Madison, Wisconsin, tornadoes are the natural disaster to fear. When we moved to the Midwest, my parents obediently learned the difference between a tornado watch and a tornado warning, the best place to be in the house during a tornado, the sound of a tornado compared to an ordinary thunderstorm, and how to know when to leave your shelter.

A yellow tornado siren stood down the street from our house, by the railroad tracks, and on several nights every summer Dorie and I woke to my parents carrying or ushering us down to the basement as the sirens wailed in the wind. The cozy time with Mom and Dad, the treat of sleeping in a sleeping bag, and the sense of fear were exhilarating. We were scared together against the downstairs bathtub. I half tried to sleep and half tried to stay awake, feeling small compared to the storm outside. Maybe if we went upstairs for something, the top of the house would be blown away before we came down again. Maybe all that would be left of our possessions was in that bathroom. Maybe morning would never come. The dangers were thrilling. Feeling afraid made me feel strong—and these dangers were *possible* but not *likely*.

The night before my seventh birthday, storms whipped around our house as we huddled downstairs for one of the first tornado warnings of the season. The next morning, our house and trees stood, but Barneveld, a small town a few miles from Madison, was gone. We saw on the news where the town used to be. A tornado had leveled it, taken it, left the land barren as it once was. I pictured the tornado skipping over us, not choosing us this time.

Years later when I was in high school I stayed home with our dog, Manna, while my parents drove my sister out to college in Virginia. It was my first time home alone overnight and I felt tall with freedom and nervousness. The afternoon they left, a summer storm came, and though it was only simple thunder, I took Manna to the basement bathroom and read, because that was the room where we had been safe from the dangers of the world before. I thought about how strong I used to feel, cozy here with my family, and I realized I didn't want that kind of strength anymore. I wanted my family home, on sunny days, our routines crowded around us. I pulled Manna next to me against the tub, waiting for the storm to bring a deeper green outside, waiting for a courage to descend as if I could tug it straight from the sky.

⊰⊱

The evening of my parents' tenth-anniversary dinner, the babysitter canceled. On the fringe of being old enough to stay by ourselves, Dorie and I assured our parents that we would be fine while they went out. Armed with the phone numbers for the restaurant, fire department, police department, doctors, and poison control center, we settled in for an uneventful evening having a picnic on the floor in our bedroom.

It wasn't long after my parents closed the door behind them that we decided we wouldn't *leave* the bedroom until they got back. The house was suddenly too creaky and too quiet at the same time. So when we needed a fork, we faced a dilemma. Who would go down the hallway to the kitchen? Who would open the door, not knowing what might be out there?

I was the one who ventured out to get that fork, then scurried back to the room to fits of laughing and more dessert. This was courage, I understood; this was what it meant to be *brave*. Courage was also what I needed to jump into the swimming pool or ride my bike down Whitcomb

Drive. It was the moment before making the choice to move, the nub of desire to be on the other side of what scared me.

Not long after my first babysitter-less night, I had surgery to remove a growth from my arm—an ugly brown oval I'd had from birth and had grown used to. "Dr. Flannery called," my mom explained to me, "and she and another doctor talked, and they think the best thing to do would be to take it off." I felt quiet inside, a silence that needs to be alone to think itself through. All I could do to express this was to go back to play.

I did not know that the doctors thought the growth might be cancerous or how concerned my parents must have been to have their daughter going in for surgery. My mom and I read numerous library books about hospitals and doctors—Danny was cross-eyed but now he can play baseball; Karen got a lot of sore throats but now she's hardly ever sick; Mommy went to the hospital and came home with a baby brother. The stories and photographs fascinated me. Would I get to wear those bright pajamas?

Then several days before the surgery, Dorie and I were playing with our dollhouses when my mom brought in a finger-puppet mouse my aunt had sent me. *Hmmmm. Apparently when one has surgery, one receives gifts. This might not be a bad situation.*

The night before surgery, my sister and I cuddled on either side of my dad as he read from a Chesapeake Bay mystery. I held tightly to Love Puppy, the stuffed dog my parents had given me to take to the hospital. Our bedtime routine was normal, but oh, this scary feeling I had. I was alone in having this surgery; my family couldn't come in with me. I had sensed the magnitude of this when my dad had prayed out loud about the next morning. That night, I didn't want him to stop reading.

The next day when we checked into the hospital, a nurse gave Love Puppy a hospital bracelet with her name on it, just like I had. Later, the doctors told me to count backwards from ten and then I woke up and it was over and my mouth was a glob of cotton and my mom—the only person who would know I needed water without me asking for it—wasn't there.

I was a "brave girl" to go through surgery, my teacher said, but the sling and the bandage were inconvenient and embarrassing, and I wore a painful, tight jacket at night to keep the swelling of the incision down. No common storm was driving the city to its basements; I saw that being special was a thin line away from being alone.

I remember standing by myself in my parents' bedroom one evening after the surgery, in front of the mirror that kept guard over my mom's dresser and all its mom-things like necklaces and safety pins. I cried when I thought of the doctor taking the stitches out, leaving this red gash by my shoulder. My arm that had been such a good companion was now against me and no one was saying I could go back to how things were or sidestep the dread I had of more pain.

I did not know then that I was getting stronger, that fear unearths the faith in us. Every doctor's appointment and painful night and teasing was carving out a resilience without my choosing. Later I would learn the pink quietness that memory takes when looking back on what we feared, the smooth courage of a scar.

One Sunday at church I heard Grace Wallace, a beautiful, older faith pillar among us, ask for prayers for someone who had recently "received the Lord." As people nodded and affirmed the request and the thanksgiving, my mind hung on her words. *How does she know that makes any difference?* The question pinned me in time, cold on a Sunday morning. I don't remember thinking about surgeries or storms. If there was a God, it was possible that He could fit in with those things. But how did Grace Wallace, in the front row of Elim Baptist Church, believe that Jesus Christ once lived and that it mattered if someone believed He lived? All I had accepted to that point came to a standstill. I would need to work this out, trembling. I would need to wait and see if I believed it too.

"Working out our faith" seems the only phrase that fits. Looking it over, putting it down, and then searching desperately for where we left it. As a child, all this working it out for me went on as I got ready for school or burst with anger at my sister or prayed secret prayers into a gold-edged journal. Faith in God began to take courage. It was risky, a leap into the pool. *How do I know this is true?* I searched for a place where I was contained again, where I felt strong because I was afraid.

I sorted my questions out without recognizing what I was doing, storing understandings away as mysteries I wanted to pursue. Even as I questioned whether a God was there, I started writing down Bible verses in my flowery notebook, writing them on index cards, writing them on slips of paper I put by my bed at night. I read every verse with a first-time awe and a gnawing in my soul.

"Now faith is being sure of what we hope for and certain of what we do not see," I wrote on a square of blue paper the night before I was to find out if I passed my algebra test in eighth grade. Coming across that verse offered clarity for my most significant trouble at the time. *God wants me to believe that He is taking care of me.* It was only a glimpse of God, but what can we do but form our view from glimpses? Faith is built on memories of blue-paper-trust, that brief belief that God is shaped perfectly for the prayers inside us.

<hr/>

That same year I entered the pull and confusion of adolescence, wondering how to stoke up courage for a suddenly foreign world. I watched others do so easily what I feared—go on dates, joke around in class, stand up to speak in front of strangers—and yet I felt courageous for getting to school every morning, walking through halls of people who I felt sure were giggling about me, being alone in the house on evenings when the corners held darkness and I feared even myself.

Courage had to be more than willing myself to jump in the water or to keep my eyes on my dad at the bottom of the hill, pedaling, pedaling, keep going straight. It meant having a faith that something else might be bigger than my fear.

The small church I attended while I was growing up met in a YMCA. The worship service was held in the gym, Sunday school in the weight rooms, and during coffee break the handful of children raced through the hallways by the racquet ball courts or played with the aerobic mats that were in the hall closet next to the Easter banners.

One Christmas, we children acted out the Nativity scene while Kris Hopkins sang a solo. Now, the advantage to being in a small church at Christmas is that every child gets a fairly significant role in the Christmas play. We had no rocks, no background stars, no sheep still in the field. I was Mary that year, and my baby doll Holly with the brushable black curls was Jesus. For days before that Sunday I practiced gazing lovingly down at my babe in arms. The song was over too soon for my taste as the kneeling mother of God.

The next year we had no play or Nativity scene, but every Sunday a family went up front to light the next candle in the Advent wreath. When it was my family's week, my parents talked to us about what would happen. My dad was going to pray, my mom was going to read from Scripture, and my sister was going to say something about the Advent candle we were lighting. Then I was to take that week's candle and light it by tipping it to the candle that was already lit from the week before.

As we practiced our routine at home, I froze at my part. "I can't do it," I told my parents. I thought of those people we knew so well sitting around me in their orange and blue metal chairs. I cried. I thought of how silent it would be as I tipped the candle. I cried some more. "I *can't.*"

My mom made a deal with me that if I couldn't light the candle on Sunday, she would do it. I just needed to stand up there. When the candle morning came, we went up front at the right time and stood behind the wreath. I stared at the candle instead of the people around us. My dad prayed. My mom read from the Bible. As Dorie was saying her lines, it struck me, *All I have to do is light the candle.* It suddenly seemed very simple. This wasn't a matter of thinking about the people around me or trying to look spiritual or keeping my hand steady. All I had to do was take one candle and tip it to another. When my sister stopped speaking, my mom looked at me and I took that candle and I lit it. That was it. That was the next thing to do. *I didn't even need to not be scared,* I thought as we returned to our seats.

I'd forgotten about this until years later when lighting an Advent candle in front of fifty people seemed a small task compared to navigating the stretch of future in front of me. I was making the unexpected decision about whether to move from Illinois, which seemed safe but boring, to the complete unknown of Colorado. The memory of standing in a gym at Christmastime came like a small gift. *I just need to do the next thing. I don't need to analyze what I don't know or pray through everything that may or may not happen.* God was filling that moment alone, doing the next thing with me, and I felt as peaceful about moving to Colorado as I did about lighting that candle. Faith seemed simple, a child's bite.

I would need more courage than I had imagined to travel through the loneliness of a new land. I melted into my apartment after work every day, sometimes too tired from deadlines and relationships to eat or even turn on the lights in the living room. It took more faith to press on in my job than it did to move; God appeared to be everywhere but in the moment I was living.

As I wondered what I'd gotten myself into by doing the next thing, an underground faith began to flow—not the faith of bravery or willpower or endurance but the faith of leaning against my dad during a tornado warning and falling asleep. I had to choose this faith again and again, choose to let something grow within me at its own rhythm while life raged around me, also at a rhythm beyond my control. I learned how messy faith is, how quickly dirtied, how small. I saw perfect love casting out fear constantly in me, as if bailing out a boat or escorting someone out of the house who keeps sneaking back in.

Several months after I moved to Colorado, I went to a movie alone one Saturday night, an experience that always reminds me of sitting at a table for two with only a novel. The movie was uneven and harsh, and only a handful of couples were in the theater. It was late when I got home, but I wasn't ready for sleep. Instead I sat in my living room with light coming only from the kitchen nearby and thought about everything, the gulp of the world, and nothing, a restful blankness, at the same time.

This is the moment I need courage for, I thought. *The only one.* Moving, like riding my bike, like jumping into the pool, like prayer, was a piece towards courage, a piece towards a greater sense of God's companionship. *We moved here together. We're alone together tonight.* I wanted to trust that God's love would be enough for me, and the only way to trust was to remember. *All I need to know right now is that Your promises have been true in the past.*

Faith was many seeds I struggled to hold, believing that mountains would move as they had in the past, rising up before me, a beauty ready to be touched. A courage I could not see glowed steady on its own, the light of a small, determined flame.

CHAPTER EIGHT

One Thing: Passion

In elementary school I believed I would grow up to be an actress. And a singer. And a dancer on the side. Julie Andrews without the height. I remember running into the laundry room one afternoon to tell my mom about this plan. Now, my mom was not a mom who said, "You can be anything you want to be." She said, "You'll be just the right person. But you're better at some things than others. You can't be *anything* you want to be."

This response did not fit into my definition of good mothering at the time. "You're not supposed to say that!" I told her as she transferred clothes to the dryer. "I *am* going to be an actress and I *know* it and you're supposed to *believe* me!"

"OK, I'm sorry, honey."

So my laundry-room revelation was met with support for me as a person but not applause for the idea itself; I was undaunted. I was the star of one-girl plays after dinner, having finished my meal roughly an hour before the adults did, sometimes before we finished praying for it. I entertained dinner guests who were polite and amused. I was the Irish washerwoman in a fourth-grade skit—my first and last audition to win. I was Cinderella in our living room for numerous productions of a musical version of the fairy tale, while my sister played the entirety of the remaining cast. I had only two costume changes—from an old dress and bare feet to a new dress with red-sequined heels, then back to the old dress. Dorie, on the other hand, was frequently running to and from the dining room to change from the stepsister to the bugler to the fairy godmother to the stepmother to the prince. My parents clapped from the sofa every time we reached the last scene where my sister-prince knelt in front of me to propose by the imaginary fireplace of my poverty.

When we were bored with Cinderella, my sister and I put on Shel Silverstein poetry readings, sometimes in front of a mirror if no parent was available to watch. *I am writing from inside a lion. . . .* I loved the story of Clooney the Clown, who couldn't make people laugh until the day he started to cry and everyone thought he was funny.

In later elementary school I was Marta in "So Long, Farewell" at a choir concert. Emily, as Gretl, sang the last line of the song before all of us von Trapp children filed off stage. At the spring concert the year before, Emily and I sang with gusto a duet of our own Easter version of "Silver Bells." *City sidewalks, busy sidewalks, dressed in Easter-egg style. . . .*

I did not see myself as the youngest child wanting attention, as a poor actor with a hollow voice. My desire to perform wasn't as great as my desire to be known. For all this time I felt something bursting inside me, I felt a soul rising up. I was headed in one direction, a direction that I could not yet name but that was defining me. *I am special, I am alive, nothing matters but this one thing that is out there waiting for me.* I had the passion to live extravagantly in an accepting little world, and I was watching myself just as my small audiences were.

We had a "question jar" in my family as I was growing up, a wooden canister with a blue ceramic top. Anybody could put questions in it during the week, and we would talk about them at dinner on special question-jar nights. I had the most questions, mainly because I was usually the first to finish dinner and was easily bored. As the rest of my family labored through their meal, I scribbled questions down on slips of paper until the question jar's lid barely stayed on. "Did Adam have a belly button?" "Why was God mean in the Old Testament?" "Do you wish you'd had a boy instead of me?" My parents offered answers or at least some musings and often my sister joined in. Every once in a while, my dad added a question in his flat scrawl: "Do you think I should go back to taking piano lessons?" "What would you like to do for vacation this summer?"

Questions and imaginings burst out of me as passion itself asked, *What if? What if I lived on the moon? What if horses could fly? What if Manna and I were invisible and could walk down the street with no one knowing?* These were the kinds of questions God once used to start the world, the wonderings that rolled out the elaborate grass I felt, cool under my toes.

I saw passion in my parents when they leaned in toward the one thing in front of them, sunk themselves into a day or a decision like children coming home to rest. My mom would disappear for an all-day painting workshop. When she returned, she put her new canvas on top of the refrigerator to dry. My dad would sit outside in the spring, reading, a stack of books and highlighters on the deck next to him. He later brought the books to the dinner table with a gush of quotes and ideas to tell my mom. My mom would laugh with friends or get angry and slam the bedroom door. On August days my dad would pick a tomato from the garden and eat it over the sink, salt and spray, as if to swallow the garden itself, let the summer roll over him in waves. This kind of living was more real to me than the click of my dad's suitcase before he left for work, the list of calls my mom needed to make, the busy weekend afternoons when the rest of my family seemed too tired for questions.

Only when I was sick as a child did my own questions die away. Numerous childhood memories float around staying home from school, the sick quilt being pulled down from the bathroom closet, the sound of my mom swallowing as I leaned against her neck. A frequent prescription was a thick, banana-flavored medicine that my sister tried to get me to drink by running around the dining room table until I took it. Sicknesses, doctor's appointments, and medicines were accepted accents of elementary school and summer vacations.

My cousin Brent carried me in and out of the doctor's office one spring break when I got strep throat while we were visiting my dad's family in Pennsylvania. When we got back to my aunt and uncle's, my mom made a bed for me out of Charlie Brown sheets on the sofa and stayed with me while the rest of the family went to the zoo. I slept and took medicine and rallied enough strength to play the occasional game of Pac-Man, savoring luscious hours with my mom alone and hoping the zoo excursion would extend into the evening. By the time my family returned, I was slipping into those cottony hours of sickness before bedtime, when everyone seems too alive and loud on the other side of my fog and the night stretches restless and lonely.

The next morning, Easter, a broken fever woke me as if looking for someone to celebrate with. The abandon, the strength! I swallowed without pain for the first time in days, that glorious childhood feeling. The medicine was working. The world was righted for play. Family cheers erupted from the breakfast table as I came down the stairs. I pounced on the basket waiting at my place, tearing off the hollow head of my chocolate bunny and comparing

"Hello Kitty" notepads with my sister in the joy of a child who believes all sicknesses are brief. And passion breaks through the flatness of fever as if to say, *Are you ready to live with desire again? Are you ready to wake up?*

Every week for eleven years in childhood I took piano lessons from Mrs. Jones. Mrs. Jones held a recital at the end of every school year and required all her students to memorize their recital pieces. My first recital piece, at the age of six, was "March of the Gingerbread Men." Looking out the window of the station wagon on the way to the recital, I experienced for the first time that shivery, closed-eyes fear of failure. *What if I forgot the notes? What if people laugh?* I looked down at the brown and white gingerbread men marching across the cover of my sheet music; we were supposed to bring the music in case we needed it. *What if my mom has to bring the music up to me because I can't remember what to play?* My sister, more experienced with this sort of thing, sat calmly beside me in the car.

I was the second to play that year, since Mrs. Jones arranged her students from youngest to oldest. The younger children were sometimes done in less than a minute or two, while the older high schoolers—those tall, secure, perfect high schoolers—played long and complicated pieces that bored me.

I don't remember the actual playing of "March of the Gingerbread Men," but I remember getting off the piano bench and bowing as Mrs. Jones had taught us. I was so tickled that I had remembered the piece and people clapped and I could sit next to my parents for the rest of the recital. Mrs. Jones sat in one of the back seats clapping and smiling, tickled as well. We had cookies and punch and congratulations afterward. Driving home that afternoon, I was sure all the world would be mine.

My second year I played "Squirrels in a Nut Tree," another successful performance, and then the songs blend together in my mind, each one requiring a longer wait at the recital because I was a year older and needed to sit through the bouncy pieces of the five- and six-year-olds who wiggled their way on and off that piano bench.

My senior year in high school, I was not the best student at the recital, but I was finally the oldest, the last to play. I was going to play "Clair de Lune" and a jazz piece. Mrs. Jones told us older students to practice the pieces in our minds, backwards, before we sat down to play them, but instead I pictured myself rising up off that piano bench to bow after my triumphant final chord, the faces of first and second graders in the audience wide-eyed at the flourish of my fingers.

So when I blanked out in the middle of the jazz piece and had to begin again and then couldn't remember how "Clair de Lune" even *started*, the room felt despairingly silent, Mrs. Jones the most silent of all in the back row, waiting. I closed my eyes and pictured the sheet music on the chair next to my mom, pictured what the first measure would be if I were to open those pages. All thoughts of playing passionately faded into the sudden need to get through that song. I ended up starting somewhere in the first third of the piece, the only thread of memory sticking out in my mind to pull on. The rest of the piece unraveled from my fingers and I finished, and I bowed, and Mrs. Jones came up to hug me, to say good-bye. Later, over punch and cookies, I burst into tears next to her.

"I don't know why you're crying," she said. "You did fine." But I could not shake from my memory the swirl of rustling papers and waiting and sweat. The risk of living extravagantly loomed greater than I'd understood. What if that one thing inside me faded to mist, could no longer carry me into the future? Passion did not seem worth the cost of that shy and apologetic bow.

One of my favorite records as I was growing up had the story of Noah on one side and the story of Joseph on the other. I loved lying on my stomach on the living room floor by the record player, looking at the album cover as the storyteller's voice moved me through well-known words. Joseph's story was my favorite. Over and over, I heard of the colored coat and the cupbearer and Joseph turning away so those he loved could not see his sadness and joy. I loved the fact that he was too loud sometimes, that he didn't fit in, that he cried. All his choices seemed to lean towards a purpose he never forgot.

Already at this point in life, my orderly personality was showing itself. I alphabetized my comic books, cut out articles from the *Smithsonian* and filed them by category without reading them. I did not like to eat my Halloween candy—what if I wanted it later? I restrained myself from reading too much at night so I would have more of the book left in the morning. Yet it bothered me that I could not turn away to cry, as Joseph did, in the midst of an ordered and unemotional world.

It was at a summer family camp in high school that passion again awakened that unquestioned longing for risk I'd had as a little girl. I had just returned from a high school trip to France that had fallen far from the life and excitement I thought it would bring. The awkward, the smart, the popular—we were together on common ground. But the new lands of Europe and adolescent behavior around me left me confused and lonely.

When I arrived home, my mom picked me up at the airport and we drove to the camp where my dad and sister were already staying. The first night there, I stood in an assembly room listening to college students around me belt out hymns and spiritual choruses as if they were trying to pull God down from heaven. It was too much. I slipped out the back door and went down to the lake, where I shook out a hundred tears. How could I ever express what I thought of God and bear it? How do any of us carry the weight of being created in the image of Someone holy?

My mom found me by the lake, and when she asked me what was wrong, all I could say, in all-or-nothing teenage fashion, was "I'm going to do *anything* for God," before melting into tears again. If I was grieving anything then, it was my insufficiency, it was my embarrassment at wanting to fit in too much, it was how distant I was from Someone I wanted to be close to.

As many defining moments are, though, that evening was a secret between God and a deeper soul in me than I knew. God was reminding me of the passion I once had to live towards one thing alone, to follow not a specific calling as much as a sense of purpose. God was creating again the desire to live extravagantly despite the risk, to make promises I could never meet on the skeleton of my own strength, to step recklessly into the abundance of a future I had yet to know.

Maybe it took extreme emotion and conviction to commit to splurging myself on God, because my first inclination is still to hoard—information, time, money, Halloween candy. The story of the woman pouring perfume at Jesus' feet always makes me uncomfortable, though I nod with the others in church when the story is told. I don't know if I would have given up that much perfume, if I would have wiped his feet without thinking of what was lost. I rarely desire one thing so much that I will lose the rest lavishly.

So I build toward greater passion with the moments I understand, feeling that pulse towards life in food set in front of me, the pouring of cake batter, the smell of spices. I find passion in prayers I wake up praying on days that frighten me, a morning desperation of *God, this is what I need to know of You today.* Passion is also my husband waiting for me at the end of a long airport terminal and the sound of my nephew's voice answering the phone: "Hi! It's me! Nathan!" I am passionate when I journal at the end of the day, pull words to me like covers tucked under my chin, or save one day a week to waste. Passion is the art of living toward one thing, the freedom to let the lesser choices fade.

The first Sunday I took Communion I was sitting on an orange chair in the aerobics room at the west side Madison Y, the sanctuary of our church. My dad was leading hymns that day, conducting us with the same fervor he had when he conducted to an empty living room on Saturday afternoons. I was too old to stand on the chair next to my mom as we sang but too young to understand many of the long words in the hymnbook. So I had time to look around and think.

The silver Communion trays and round loaf of bread sat by the pulpit like a wizened couple waiting to speak. I knew that Lisa Schulz made bread for Communion in her kitchen at home and this interested me. Somewhere between her house and our sanctuary, it became special bread.

I paid attention to the pastor's words about breaking this bread and drinking this cup, and though I'd been told what it all meant, I had many questions. Was Jesus really thinking of me when He said these things? What does it mean to do something because we remember Him?

After the pastor gave out the juice and bread, I swung my legs under my chair and looked around, not sure if I should go ahead and eat or not. Several other children in the congregation were taking Communion for the first time that day as well. We looked at each other and tried not to giggle, but the silence of the room stilled us as the adults slowly, intentionally, slid the grape juice and bread into their mouths. For a moment, it was the only thing that mattered.

Communion Sundays became routine after awhile. At the church I attended in high school, we went to the front of the sanctuary to receive the elements—moms holding babies, a husband with his hand on his wife's shoulder, children who reached up to take the wafer from the plate. It was a terribly self-conscious walk for a teenager but looking back, I like the sense of exposure I felt. It is a vulnerable thing to stand up and say we need the mercy of God.

In France, I would take Mass not knowing I wasn't supposed to, and on a vacation years later I would sip sharp wine from a heavy cup and pass it on. In college and graduate school I again walked up front as music played, feeling unnoticed, every church service the step before a pale and silent Sunday afternoon.

After I got married, my husband and I visited many churches with their respective Communion traditions as we tried to figure out what it meant to belong to a church as a couple. Then the growing familiarity of a church home, where people touch your arm as you pass because you are known. I look at faces around me and see that Communion is the beat beneath a range of emotions and desire and obedience on Sunday mornings. It is a reminder of recklessness that speaks through our fevered haze and cautioned living.

After hundreds of Communion services, the words and tastes sometimes still surprise me, though rarely when I try to be surprised. *The body of Christ, broken for you.* This is a feast prepared, this is the quiet exuberance of risk. *Therefore, we proclaim the mystery of faith.* This is the celebration of living in one direction, the call to respond to another's passionate choice. And Jesus says with a purpose only sacrifice can bring, *Take and eat.*

CHAPTER NINE

First Words: Voice

The fall my sister went to kindergarten, my parents were planning to take me to a hearing specialist. I was two and a half and my vocabulary consisted of *Ma, Da,* and *juice.* My sister interpreted the rest of my babbles, neither of us expressing alarm at my limited speech.

It was the day Dorie got on her first kindergarten bus, as my mom and I watched from the front porch, that I looked at my mom and said, "When I'm five years old, I'm going to go to kindergarten too."

Was it a shock to feel words in my mouth and see someone understand them? I wonder if someday I will be granted the gift of knowing what drove me to take my collection of unspoken words and start saying them. I do know, almost as if I remember it, that I had many words to say before I spoke, but I chose to hold them in.

Perhaps I sensed that once I chose to have a voice, I risked losing it.

In the days that followed this linguistic revolution, a tumble of words began to come, my new mouth sorting and forming syllables and sentences. I soon learned that my voice was important. People wanted me to speak. They asked me questions and they seemed pleased to get words out of me. Later I would learn that only the newest children in the world, in fact, are allowed the wonder of not speaking. If we choose silence beyond those years or months, we are called withdrawn, diseased, strange, perhaps even religious.

I learned this because I grew up being told I was shy. Though I might be chatty at home, around strangers I was decidedly quiet. "I'm not shy," I wanted to say. "I just don't need to talk right now." Sometimes I wondered why other people felt the need to talk so *much*. I saw that my friends' parents were uncomfortable with my silence at the dinner table or at birthday parties, but I didn't feel the need to respond to their questions. Instead, I drew pictures in art class with people's eyes large and round, watching, and their mouths a closed afterthought.

When I did express myself, it seemed to surprise people. One lunch period in first grade I got left behind in the classroom as the rest of the class filed down to the cafeteria. "And then I heard this scream," Miss Sawyer told my mom after school as I stood by the hallway bench. She seemed both concerned and amused, startled at this mute six-year-old alerting the hallway to her needs. *What else was I supposed to do?* I wondered. I was alone and I didn't know if anyone knew I was in there. I screamed. It didn't seem unlike me at all. With a child's comprehension, I began to realize that I wasn't fully understood. My thoughts and emotions were mine, not my parents' or my teachers'. I could make my voice loud or I could refuse to make it move at all. Only God knew all I might say. I was my own secret.

When I learned how to form written letters, I began to throw words to paper to see if I could be my secret there. Like most children, I wrote about animals: blue jays and skunks and ducks, a parade of puppies, and the occasional kitten. Traces of sadness appeared in what I wrote, and this seemed to be part of telling the secret. I have a copy of an assignment in first grade that was designed to teach students how some letters rose above the middle line and some sank below the bottom line. A story was already started on the newsprint paper so we could see how different letters worked. "Jip was happy. He . . .," the printed words said next to a drawing of a dog. The rest of the space was left for the student. " . . . was sad too," I continued in my section.

I enjoyed seeing how my voice could change things, how my ideas and words could create a picture crisp and new. In second grade, I wrote stories in a notebook with a cloth cover and gave it to my teacher after school. When I didn't know how to finish a story, I made it a "finish your own," until my mom suggested that was a cop-out. I wrote poems for the school newspaper about things I didn't know I cared about and wrote down adventures I almost thought I had been in. I saw that writing was encouraged at school but in most of life, people still wanted me to talk more.

When I did speak, my voice came out more odd and unpredictable than I wanted it to, but others seemed pleased. Then in third grade I had my first haunting experience with my own words. Emily and I were playing Hangman in our classroom and it was my turn to make up the puzzle. "Ellen doesn't like it when we play together" was my offering. Just as Emily solved it, I saw that Ellen was standing behind us. She looked at me and walked away. I felt myself grow hot and still. That night my mom and I went to feed the next door cats, Yabut and Motherly, because our neighbor, Mrs. Brown, was out of town. I told my mom without looking at her about the Hangman game. We walked outside and sat on the porch. I played with a caterpillar.

"When I was about your age," my mom said, "I went over to Shirley Ashcroft's house and wrote, 'Nobody likes Shirley' in chalk on the sidewalk in front of her driveway." I was shocked. I pictured my mom—as my mom—scribbling out words and running home. I don't remember what else she said that evening, but I was comforted that she, too, had once had an initiation into the strength of voice.

My experience with Ellen unsettled me. I resented the fizz of my own words. It seemed too much for God to ask a person to hold, this voice that could hurt and destroy. I wanted it to hollow out, to disappear, but it kept jolting me forward, part of a throng of voices startled to be talking so loudly.

Like most teenagers, I tried out my voice in different ways in high school, wishing it sounded more powerful than it did. I was in a bad play my sophomore year—a Greek myth reset in modern times with much of the dialogue dependent on the audience knowing obscure musical numbers from the seventies. "We've seen them, we've seen the ships!" was my line, as I ran into the theater carrying a bucket with my friend Amanda. "They're going to go to Troy!" Amanda added. For the remaining hour and a half of the play, I spent most of my time backstage, listening for the "chorus" cues when I would need to venture out again into harsh light.

That was the last play I wanted to be in, which surprised me. I had watched my sister go through the drama department—she was the screaming girl at the opening of *The Crucible,* the hard-nosed lawyer in *The Night of January 16*[th]—and I was sure I could do that too. The idea of screaming and being respected for it, or acting tough and being accepted, was appealing to me. But when I got there, I found that my voice sounded the same as it did off-stage: small, tentative, and a little bored.

I tried out Pressions, the after-school writing club run by Mr. Rodriguez. Mr. Rod, as the "in" writers called him, had long hair, a black goatee, a large chain of keys hooked to his belt, a caustic sense of humor, and a respect for teenagers trying to figure out who they were. He introduced us to *Romeo and Juliet, The Pearl,* the five-paragraph essay, and how to negotiate the halls of an unkind high school. We loved him.

Pressions met once a week in the English lab near Mr. Rod's classroom. A small group of us sat around reading each others' poetry and short stories and accentuating our drifting nature as much as possible. I was the "good girl" who was drifting only minimally and didn't often wear all-black. The other students accepted me because Mr. Rod did and because I was there, writing poems with titles like "Bittersweet," "Paranoia," "Disgusting World," "Indifferent," "When Snow White and the Beav Die," and, of course, "Fear," where I contemplated the tension between the fear of melting and the fear of grass. Through pages of writing and weeks of late-afternoon critique, I explored how to name the pool of emotion I had recently fallen into. Mr. Rod explored with me, making scrawling green notes on thick printer paper, notes that I still take out to read every now and then.

My English teachers from that year on helped me think about my voice, and for all the pain of adolescence sometimes I still want to go back to their classrooms after school and sit down to talk. They gave the assignments they'd been giving for decades, but they made me feel that when I sat down to write an essay on *Jane Eyre,* I was the first one to put words together in such a way about Mr. Rochester and Thornfield and the dark attics of our lives. *Jane gains confidence and realizes that she has a right to speak with a voice that is regarded as significant and equal.* They let the blank page fascinate me.

During this time I started to write in my laptop journal, pulling it toward me in my pink recliner in the most private hours I could find, either early in the morning or late at night. What I most wanted to write were thoughts directed to God, a sorting out of disagreements I was having with God and questions about who God wanted me to be.

The voice that was unsettling or boring in waking life was alive when I prayed out quiet or angry words single-spaced in front of me. I remembered the feeling of learning to read, when I would sit at the typewriter in my dad's study and plunk out all the words I knew how to spell: *car, toe, bat, hat, cat* . . . a key at a time. *This is what I know, these are the small learnings I want to look at.* God used my own voice to increase my understanding of who God was. My words had a little more faith than I did.

⋈

In college I liked, for reasons I could not express, the verse in the book of Isaiah, "A voice says, 'Cry out.' And I said, 'What shall I cry?' " I wanted to take the voice I was learning in private prayers and speak it aloud, but whenever I tried to carry the secret sense of my room into the open, it evaporated. My mind was speechless and cold around other people.

One afternoon in college I sat in my dorm room with my roommate, practicing for an upcoming poetry reading. When I got to the end of my poem about gold coins, Carolyn stared at me. "It's good," she said, trying to encourage. "But you have no inflection in your voice." I could hear that she was right. These secret feelings—how do I cadence them? How do I give life to words when I stand in front of strangers?

I sat at the desk in my room at night, typing out what I knew in my journal, prayers the equivalent of *car, nap, dog,* that someday might string together into what I meant to say.

⋯⋯✕⋯⋯

After college, I rented two rooms in a basement near my graduate school. I spent most of my waking time in the non-bedroom, where I sat in my recliner to eat, study, read, and watch *Little House on the Prairie* reruns.

It was the fall after my parents moved from my childhood home, my sister got married, and I graduated from college, changed jobs, and moved away from friends. Even the bookstore where I used to work in Madison was moving. All I once could visit had tilted or disappeared.

Hungry for someone to share my space during that time, I realized how intimate it is for a person to come into someone else's room and sit on the bed. The way my parents used to come in at night and sit next to me rubbing my back, or lean against the wall and talk when I was having a bad day. The way Emily used to jump on my bed when we played after school, the way my friend Deb plopped down in my dorm room on college afternoons. This comfort, this familiarity. *I want to be with you.* It was someone saying my name with ease, calling to me or whispering her secrets. *I know you.*

My recliner was destined to be my prayer space for that time, but my prayers were prayers of silence. I wrapped myself in that chair and didn't realize when an hour went by. I was in a suspended staleness, a quiet thicker than any I'd known before. Depression was a room alone.

I did have a companion in waiting. I was a caregiver for my landlord's baby boy who was two weeks old when I moved in. Davis and I spent hours together playing on the floor, sleeping on the sofa, walking to and from the library, laughing.

I had found someone who heard me when I didn't speak and didn't ask me to speak more. I had also found someone I could relate to, because as Davis grew, he seemed disinclined to speak any words at all. (Like me, Davis had three older people speaking *for* him.) "Yup, he's a late talker," his dad declared, worry in his voice. Davis smiled, oblivious to all the talk about his lack of talking.

I was proud of Davis's silence even as I fed him words and named his food and toys. *Keep it while you can. It's a rare thing for someone to truly want to hear you.* He was unconcerned with not knowing where his voice was. So in silence we were each other's peace.

During this time I went back to visit Madison for a couple of weeks, staying with friends because my parents' home was now owned by a strange family with toddler toys in the yard, an old bike leaning against our hide-and-seek homebase rock. Soon after I arrived, I dropped some friends off at the airport early one morning so I could borrow their car. It was dark and cold as I drove down University and realized that ice was growing too thick on the windshield for me to see where I was going.

I pulled into the parking lot of the bookstore where I used to work, its storefront in transition to whatever it would be next. I felt so in transition myself that I sat there, in employee parking, for several minutes, not knowing how to get the back defroster to work or what to do with the rest of my life. The sun was starting to rise, which brought joy only for the situation at hand. When the ice began sliding off the windows, I was so relieved that I drove away without a look back or any thoughts to my future, although that five minutes stands white and clear in my mind.

When I returned to Illinois, both Davis and I would begin to name things, Davis to much applause, while I spoke more privately. Prayers began to come again and I said them as they came, opened my fingers like a baby awake. *God has been here,* I thought, *though I was not aware of it. God will give the silent times a voice worth hearing.*

<hr />

The Christmas of my third-grade year, our city symphony held a contest for young songwriters. The winners had their songs performed by the symphony and broadcast on the radio. With my growing knowledge of music accumulated from my piano lessons, I labored over a carol and sent it in. "Christmas Song," as I titled it with all creativity, was one of three winners.

The night of the performance, I sat next to my mom in the dark theater and read a Choose-Your-Own-Adventure book with a pen flashlight. The concert started at 8:00, which my mom thought was rather late for elementary-school composers. But when the woman next to her gave her a disdainful look for bringing a child to the program, my mom looked her in the eye and said, "My daughter wrote one of the pieces in the second half."

It was a holiday "pops" concert and the orchestra and choir made their way through several lively Christmas carols before coming to the "Madison Students' Carols" in the program. I perked up.

I had submitted my song on a hand-drawn score, dropping down notes one at a time and filling in their bold heads as I went. "Christmas trees are all around," I'd begun the song. "Snow is covering up the ground." The carol continued for a few more lines.

I knew it so well that it rang in my head as I sat waiting for the piece to begin. The song that started to come from the choir and orchestra, though, didn't sound hand-drawn. The conductor had arranged it with flourish: trumpets, violins, cellos, the range of choir voices. It was what I had written, but it wasn't. It was rich and full and layered and took longer than a minute to sing.

The choir went through the song once and then again, then again, each time dividing into more voices, repeating different lines, finally drawing itself to a crescendo around the words of an eight-year-old sitting with a flashlight in the audience. I wiggled a bit, thinking of how these people took what I had to say and made it something majestic. I wanted to say, *Yes, that's what I meant!* Those were the chords I was trying to darken in when all I could write were single notes. That was the meaning I was feeling when all that came out were simple rhymes.

I still have the radio recording and the program from that concert, even the conductor's arrangement of my piece. I sometimes pull them out and remember how the conductor took time to find what was missing, to draw out the silences as mysteries between the notes. God, too, would shape my shy voice, give beauty to my simple offerings. And I remember that surge of chorus as I sat back against the rhythm of the evening, listening like a child just learning to name things.

CHAPTER TEN

My True Name: *Identity*

Nicole Conners lived with five brothers in a house around the corner from my family. She was beautiful, though I didn't know it at the time—red hair, freckled skin, wide smile. When we first moved to Madison, my mom and Nicole's mom sometimes took turns watching us for the afternoon, dropping us off at the other's house and driving away to do things moms do.

Nicole's dark and dirty and loving home fascinated me. Her younger brothers had smelly diapers and her oldest brother thumped in and out with friends, slamming the door behind him as her mom swung a baby on a hip and navigated through toys and cries in the living room. Mr. Conners was at his job downtown; I would later watch him walking a loyal path home from the bus stop near our house.

When Nicole and I began elementary school, our moms took turns carpooling us in the morning in their respective station wagons. Nicole usually walked to our house on the days my mom drove, her braided hair hanging over her shoulders for many years of schoolday mornings. On other days, I stood at the living room window watching for the Conners to pull up, Nicole in the back next to brothers hanging from car seats and seat belts, fruit flies to their mother's steady presence behind the steering wheel.

Nicole ate "hot lunch," which meant that her family got help in paying for lunches and also meant that she traveled in different circles than the "cold lunch" crowd. She wore homemade Halloween costumes and was smart and had the glow of a child who knows she is loved. She was my summer evening playmate and I still think of her when the days start lengthening in the spring. Hide-and-seek, freeze tag, Mother-may-I, until it was time for sleep, time to wait for summer to begin again the next day.

It was a winter morning when my mom dropped Nicole and me off at school and told me to go on while she talked to Nicole alone. It seems Nicole had been stealing money from the car's jar of change when she waited for my mom to collect me for school and get me to the car in the morning. Nicole said she was saving money to buy a Christmas present for her mother.

With a sadness, my mom told me this after school that day. The following weekend, Nicole and I shoveled the deck and then kneeled on stools on either side of my mother, learning how to make decorative wreaths. The wreath was to be the gift for Nicole's mom; the shoveling was in exchange for my mom not telling Mrs. Conners about the stolen change. *I know that person with the stolen change is not who you really are,* my mom told Nicole without words. *You are someone who makes beautiful things.*

My mom says she is still unsure if she handled things well. But that Christmas, Nicole Conners gave her mom a homemade wreath, and I gave my teacher the wreath I made, and I saw how fierce and communal grace can be when we let it name us.

⌇

My parents gave me "Grace" as a middle name, after my mother's mother. I love that name because all it asks you to do is grow into it. It named me before I knew that I needed grace or could extend it, and I needed and extended grace before I could speak my name. Yet it may take the stretch of my life to grow into Grace completely, because I keep losing the truth of who I am.

At every stage of childhood, I held back what I knew until I thought I could do it well. I talked, walked, and swam late. I was even born late, arriving in a rush one morning as if I had just made up my mind that I was ready for light.

Once words awakened in me, I wanted to use them right or not at all, and the height of using words well in elementary school was getting the letters in order. I still have the journal Mrs. Pearl made us keep in third grade, the spiral-bound notebook with Snoopy on the front. It holds all the themes of an eight-year-old life: playing with Dorie or Emily, having a snack, going to bed, and doing it all again. On occasion I wrote of being sick, finishing a book, traveling, or having a substitute teacher. I also wrote about spelling tests. If any desire came through those pages, it was to get a 100 on my spelling test—on *every* spelling test. On disappointing weeks I lamented to the wide-rule lines that I had checked the list and "I think I got one wrong."

My goals have grown up with me, but I haven't gotten far from my third-grade journal, from those early years of realizing that no matter how hard I tried, I was going to "get one wrong." I drive on roads that have torn through the homes of wildlife and listen to wars and rumors of wars with the sense that if I had lived differently, others would know peace. At some point in school or playtime I realized I did not know where to find the rightness I wanted, and others did not have it either. I wonder at the irony that without grace, I will not find the self I want to be.

When I was in second grade, someone abandoned a three-month-old beagle-mix in our Toyota. My dad, sister, and I discovered her when we went out to church one Sunday morning. "There's a dog in the car! There's a dog in the car!" my sister and I yelled to my mom as we ran back into the house. Dressed for church, my mom stopped in the hallway and said, "It's a gift from heaven!"

Manna would become a part of our family, a part of growing up. She came because we had left the car unlocked in the driveway, one of those "If anyone wants to steal this car, they can have it" situations, not expecting someone to want to *give* us something. Whoever it was locked the car on the way out.

Not having a precedent for how to handle such a situation, we went to church in our other car. "The dog in the Frylings' car" was one of the prayer requests in our small congregation that week; on the way home we bought a bag of dog food.

My mom let the puppy out when we got home and ran her around the yard. My dad (allergic) and I (terrified) kept our distance. But my mom's love for dogs is a powerful force, and I don't remember a question about whether the dog would stay for at least a little while. The Humane Society reported that no one was looking for her; the neighbors posted no signs. My dad's allergies didn't mind her puppy dander. So I was the only one left. "Have you got her, have you got her?" I scrambled onto the couch whenever she came into a room, knowing how eager she was to lick the one person who did not care to be near her. It was the week my parents had decided she and I would never get along that I cried when we left her one morning, surprising myself and sealing her presence with us. It didn't take me long after that to decide she was my most understanding friend.

"Fudge" and "Velvet" were my passionate name suggestions, neither of which went over well with the rest of the family. It was Mrs. Wrobbel, my Sunday school teacher, who suggested "Manna," a gift from the sky—which literally means, "What is it?"

I categorized the "where Manna came from" question as one of the biggest mysteries of my childhood years, right up there with trying to remember what it felt like to be unborn. When I asked my mom if we would know Manna's origins when we got to heaven, she said that we may or may not, but either way we wouldn't care by then. This was a lot for a seven-year-old to think about, the idea that not all our questions are eternal.

To lose such a gift from the sky—a gentle, loving, not very bright dog, as so many of the best dogs are—was a great fear growing up. When our dog wandered out the patio door and took herself for a walk, as she did on occasion, I panicked. *She's going to be hit by a car; she'll get lost, she'll wander out to the beltline.* All was abandoned in the effort to find the wayward dog.

My station was my bike, while my mom took the car down Hammersley. I sailed through our neighborhood streets, calling her name. *Lord,* I remember praying, *I promise I'll be good, just help us find her.* Dog treats rattled in my pocket. *God, if I've done something wrong today, please forgive me and show me where she is.* I dipped in and out of cul-de-sacs. *Lord! If You let me find her, I will never sin again!*

It was usually my mom who found Manna trotting down the side of a street. In fact, I don't remember finding her even once, which saved me from facing the deal I had made with God.

It's worth a shot, I was believing as I pedaled down Whitcomb Drive. It was simpler to promise God I would be perfect than to tell God I needed help. God at the time was my parents to the nth degree—someone who loved and disciplined me and who also knew what I was thinking and doing all the time. We were always together. God was a tenderness, a tie, Someone I was getting to know again as if we had met before but needed to be reacquainted. I was God's secret. Someday He and I together would decide to reveal me.

By the time I reached Manna-searching bike rides in junior high, I was more concerned about how I *looked* riding my bike with dog treats hanging out of my pocket than whether my moral standing would make our dog appear around the corner.

Most of my bike riding in those years was not spent searching for Manna, in fact, but for something I could not name, some definition of who I was in-between my prayers for perfection and the deeper sense I had that my self could never be right on its own. I rode for hours in and out of neighborhoods, by Emily's old apartment, past the library, around the tennis courts where I had once hated taking lessons. It was on my bike that I realized my prayers were as private as the roads I decided to twist down, no one knowing exactly where I was. As I wove through this childhood solitude, I thought about how I was taking God with me as I went. Sometimes I wondered what God thought of who I was and if it would be enough for these corners I was choosing.

When Davis, my landlords' boy, was two years old and not talking much, he still understood a lot about his wordless self. When he did something wrong—hitting, not listening, throwing a toy—he apologized by stroking my cheek. When he saw me smile, he smiled and turned back to playing. When I wanted to apologize to him for something, I stroked his cheek. He looked straight in my eyes and this startled me every time, so bold he was to acknowledge that I had failed. Yet he was back to play before I forgot the softness of his face on my hand, he'd moved on as if to say, *Yes, that's true about you. But that doesn't surprise me. It doesn't define my thoughts of you.* With each recognition of how easily we fall out of who we want to be, he reminded me of who we were, people who can live well only when we let grace identify us.

Many mornings or middays now, I sit down with my Bible and try to form words or silences out of the jumbled anxieties of the day. Muddled in the void between who I am and the true identity waiting for me, I fall back on "the Jesus Prayer," the prayer of centuries—a time frame that is somehow comforting. *Lord Jesus Christ, Son of God, have mercy on me, a sinner. Lord Jesus Christ, Son of God, have mercy on me, a sinner.* My mind begins to drift. *Lord Jesus Christ, Son of God,* I'm back to it, *have mercy on me, a sinner.* This is where God defines me, this is how I know the name God gives me.

Lord Jesus Christ. The words become a boat that I am riding on the rhythm of my breathing. I breathe out, *have mercy; in, Lord Jesus Christ.* I feel the edges of my body in the chair. I feel self-contained, detailed and small. I pull my arms in and make myself reach them out again, open my hands to the weight of air. *Lord Jesus Christ, Son of God, have mercy on me, a sinner.* And I am someone who can pray eternal thoughts of God in the first part of a minute and wonder about breakfast in the second. I am someone who has both the right and the need to ask for grace, to seek again the definition of who I am and to be startled at the truth from God: *You are now someone who makes beautiful things.*

⁂

Ask, receive. Ask again. I recently stayed for a few days at a Benedictine community. There I absorbed the music and warmth of Benedictine hospitality, laughed when I was alone in my room at the joy of such a welcome. I attended services several times, stepping into the tall church building and taking the prayer book like a gift from Brother Martin.

On my first morning there, I noticed that frequently, but sporadically, choir members genuflected while singing. Later I asked Sister Catherine about this. She smiled. "Oh, that's what we do when we make a mistake. It helps keep us focused and stay humble. You know, you can be thinking about lunch or what you need to do that day and you miss a note. It helps you get back on track." I think about this as I watch the brothers and sisters later that day. *Mistake, mistake . . . another mistake.* Heads bob inconspicuously as voices float up. A sequence of sin, confession, forgiveness.

Each person knows who she is when she fails and knows who she is called to be as she keeps singing. This is a chorus of humility and mercy, a recognition of how again and again we must live into our new, redeemed name. It reminds me of how often my weaknesses appear and how quickly I could kneel my prayers and rise again. It reminds me that when I know who I am in both weakness and grace, I offer grace to others. *Lord Jesus Christ, have mercy on me.* And he will let me ask again.

I was named after Elisa Sywulka, a missionary in Guatemala. I grew up knowing this story: When I was one year old, the Sywulkas were visiting my family in New Hampshire. When my mom went to put me down for a nap, Elisa asked if she could watch. My mom welcomed her but was surprised because Elisa had children of her own, so putting a baby to bed was not a novelty. Elisa told my mom that she wanted to watch because she felt a bond with me—not just because of our names, but because Elisa's baby gift was to pray for me every day of my first year.

Sometimes when I forget what it means to live into the good name God offers, I remember that Elisa Sywulka prayed for me every day for the first year of my life. I travel back through the prayers of my parents and grandparents and mentors, thousands of words and aches and praises expressed for my life, to a small bed of a year's prayers for a baby never met before. Even if no one had prayed for me again, I was prayed for every morning by a voice I didn't know in a country I will probably never see. I was accepted as worth praying for. I think of Elisa's eyes adjusting to a darkened baby's room and I remember that I am called to be a child, to speak who I am like an ancient chant, babble it like a language I was born knowing.

I remember, too, that in this adult world it's all right to rest at the height of the day sometimes, to close my eyes in a dim nursery with cracked light around the window and lay my head on sheets as smooth and taut as a blessing. Then I can sleep because I am prayed for, and have been, and will be, and grace is in my room, waiting like the kindness of a name.

CHAPTER ELEVEN

And Heaven to Earth Will Answer: God

I first met Mrs. Wrobbel when I darted in front of her at coffee hour between our YMCA church service and Sunday school. "You don't interrupt people like that," she said, stopping me with a hand on my shoulder. I stared up at her Styrofoam cup. "You walk *around* people when they're having a conversation." This was unlike any adult I had met before. How could she tell me what to do when she didn't even know me?

I was nervous, then, to hear that Mrs. Wrobbel would be teaching me Sunday school the next fall. In 1984, the entire elementary school Sunday school class of Elim Baptist Church was Jesse Wilson, Keith Schultz, and me. We learned quickly that Mrs. Wrobbel was tough, blunt, and wanted more than anything for us to love God.

Mrs. Wrobbel taught the Bible with the same intention that she taught children manners after church. Every week, the four of us crouched in the weight room downstairs and memorized Bible verses. We played games with Bible verses, we read stories of Bible verses, and most importantly we coursed through Mrs. Wrobbel's index cards of Bible verses. On the front of each card was a picture of a Bible story or character and a reference. ("The reference is part of the verse—you have to learn both," Mrs. Wrobbel insisted.) With the three of us in front of her, Mrs. Wrobbel flipped through those cards and we either shouted out the verses or sat in a shifty silence until she gave us a hint.

Soon we each had our own sets of cards, allowing us to practice at home. I memorized verse after verse during Sunday morning breakfasts, the car ride to and from church, school night evenings. I proudly handed over my cards to recite before each Sunday school class, hoping I could pull out from my mind what I had so recently put into it.

I did not memorize verses to learn spiritually; I memorized them for the prizes. For each set of verses we memorized, we got a reward. Jesse and Keith got the boyish prizes and I got the horse prizes. Mrs. Wrobbel's three daughters had gone through horse phases and now she passed their treasures on to me. Horse posters, horse figurines, horse pens. With materialistic greed, an innate sense of competition, and the patient work of the Holy Spirit, I collected memorized verses on one side and horse paraphernalia on the other. I lined my walls and filled my room with the fruits of my spiritual quest.

Horse phases and an unhealthy love of purple dissipate as little girls grow older, but something as real as a Bible verse is harder to shake. Somewhere in the years of trying to be better than the boys and win the most stuff, I started writing out verses and memorizing them on my own. The Psalms in particular were intriguing to me, many of their stories as rich and real in my mind as *Emily of New Moon* or *Little House in the Big Woods*. Mrs. Wrobbel taught us that when we close the Bible, face the long pages towards us, and make the tips of our thumbs meet each other across the pages, we will almost always open to the Psalms, which made them easy to find along with short to read.

I copied down Psalm 23 in a yellow flowered notebook in scrawling, just-learned cursive and believed without question that the Lord was *my* shepherd, that the bearded Jesus of Sunday school books was walking with me along still waters. Psalm 119 was all about the Bible, Mrs. Wrobbel told us, and one summer I set out to memorize the whole thing, though I never finished.

Psalm 100 was another favorite, particularly because it involved shouting. "Enter his gates with thanksgiving," my dad boomed through the aerobics-room sanctuary on Sunday mornings when he read Scripture. "And his courts with praise," we all answered, even Mrs. Wrobbel, who stood in the front row. Then Laurel Falk would play the piano as if it were an orchestra, her eyes unblinking on the page in front of her, and we would rise and sing, and I, the quiet girl standing next to my mom, would be shouting inside, as if the richest praises can also be the silent ones.

⋙⋘

I see now that Mrs. Wrobbel's eagerness, even desperation, to teach us Bible verses came from an understanding that one day soon we might not want to put those verses in our heads and the prizes we sought would be far more complicated than toys. God would change for us, for me, and would sometimes slip away. The all-knowing, all-caring shepherd of elementary school would become a capricious vending machine at times in high school, as I battered God to steady the world again for me.

I had not seen Mrs. Wrobbel for about ten years when she came to my high school graduation party and gave me a small desk clock. On the back of the clock was the reference for Psalm 32:8 (references are, after all, very important). I looked up at her, wondering if this was one of my index-card verses that I had forgotten. "I will instruct you and teach you in the way you should go; I will counsel you and watch over you," she quoted to me, smiling the smile I looked for whenever I said a reference correctly. For a reason I did not understand, she seemed pleased with me, even proud. The verse came as a promise from her hands, like a prayer from one who was familiar with praying for me.

I took those words from Scripture with me to college and I clung to the hope that God was watching over me even when I couldn't sense that God was there.

My first vacation at home during my freshman year, I dreamt that I was kneeling on the floor in a dark church sanctuary trying to put together a stained-glass window. Colored pieces were all around me, scattered before the gaping hole where the window should be. *You don't need to know how to do this,* I heard in my dream, more clear than a conscious voice. *I'll take care of putting the window back.* I woke up on Thanksgiving morning, light coming in my childhood bedroom and my family rustling in the hallway. *I will watch over you.* And so God can use dreams and the prayers we wake up with to live out the promises Scripture makes, to counsel us through presence alone, a teacher, as if mystery is sometimes enough.

Your path led through the sea, your way through the mighty waters, though your footprints were not seen. My first year of grad school I spent waiting for God to piece together a darker puzzle, my days scattered out before me without color or pattern. That year I bustled home in the winter dark from night classes and curled up with the space heater before bed to let the day unwind from my mind. Little light came into my basement rooms and every evening I wanted to sink further back into my chair, into the rough white walls behind me. Even Mrs. Wrobbel's psalms held little comfort; I stopped reading the Bible outside of class work, only because I had little energy for routine or thought beyond getting up in the morning.

Like most dark seasons, that time felt empty of change, though when I look back I realize my soul was groaning like river ice melting and those blank times held more transition than the years on either side of them. During that basement of a year I did not see the faith of generations rise up on every side of me or feel the strength of Sunday school words, but every prayer I'd let pale against the hours stood by me ready to thrive. God comes near in the times we lose God most, tender for us to find Him again.

On some nights after class I sat with the warmth of my Bible in my lap. Sometimes, to know I could, I measured my thumbs cover to cover over the pages and pulled those pages open. There were the Psalms, waiting, just as Mrs. Wrobbel had said.

⊰⊱

For years I used to underline parts of psalms and other verses I liked in my plain hardcover Bible, and I often wrote a date in the margin to remember the circumstances I was in at the time. *All my longings lie open before you, O Lord; my sighing is not hidden from you.* Now the smudged pencil dates mean little, a vague sense of where I was that year and who I was with, but they form a reminder of God's presence, a group of gray friends standing nearby to tell me *God was here.*

That basement time was a dying time, as every season of loss is, and though new life may grow from ashes, death is still the last enemy. For what if God dies? What if Mrs.

Wrobbel was wrong in her prayers for me?—in who she said God was? God is not who I think God is, not who I want God to be. But faith is telling God, *This is what I know about You now. I will act on this belief. I will act as if these things are true.* Faith is taking my harvest of Bible verses and feeling them smooth in my hands and saying, *I know these words. I choose to believe these words have power in me.*

A professor once wrote on one of my graduate school papers, *"God's strong hand is on you."* I often think of those words; sometimes I say them to others. *God's strong hand is on you.* Are you scared? Is the hand too strong? *Even in the dying times, God's strong and faithful hand is on you.*

<hr />

When my Grandpa Fryling was in Europe during World War II, he sent gifts home to my grandmother, including a box of handkerchiefs with the note, "With all my love, dearest sweetheart. Your grateful husband, Herb. Italy, July 17, 1944." My mom has the note framed in her living room not just for the intimacy it speaks of between my dad's parents but because it was written on the day she was born. In the rages of war God was bringing to life a love for a son not yet alive, though it would be years before that piece of God's faithfulness showed itself.

I have always felt a particular connection to my grandfather. We both love mashed potatoes and jokes. Tears were passed down to me from my grandfather through my father, "the Fryling tears," my grandmother says looking at my mom, both dry-eyed.

Years ago my grandfather told me, while we were sitting in my family's living room, that he carried words from the book of Nahum with him through the war. He quoted a verse to me then, his wide, curious eyes watching me, King James language warm in his voice: "The LORD is good, a strong hold in the day of trouble; and he knoweth them that trust in him." He carried those words with him then as truly as he'd carried them in his breast pocket across France and Italy, waiting to come home to his wife. "The LORD is good."

Now my grandfather is blind, a resident in a nursing home, and he and my grandmother are sleeping in different beds for the first time since those years of war. Sometimes a nurse or my grandmother wheels him down to a resident Bible study and sometimes he'll start praying there, in the middle of a lesson, and the teacher stops teaching and the residents bow their heads and my grandfather prays and then falls asleep.

I visited my grandparents last year, and as I sat holding my grandfather's hand, his fingers flat and smooth as tissue paper, it struck me that after years of war, pain, and blindness, God is one of the only things my grandfather hasn't lost. He may not remember I was here holding his hand, he can't see his room, and that night he will be so restless that the nurses will be at a loss for how to get him to sleep. He saw boxcars in Dachau, he gave up the first two years of his oldest son's life. He has now lost every friend he has had, most to death, some to lack of memory. He plays the harmonica, as he did during the war, and he still loves the taste of potatoes and gravy. But what he knows most clearly are the words of Scripture, the verses that began to weave through his thoughts as a boy. *The* LORD *is good.*

During my visit, my aunt talked to Grandpa about how he needs to go to sleep when it's night. She suggested that when he can't rest he pray for my grandma, who had been sick recently.

"Oh, I *do.*" He leaned forward, his eyebrows raised in the direction of my aunt's voice. "I pray for Roberta every day. I *never* stop praying for her." My grandfather, with the beret and the riddles and the red Ford pulling into our driveway, sits up to speak of prayer the way a toddler speaks the only word he can spell or tells how old he is going to be next month. *This I know, this is all I know.* He has decided that beyond anything else, God will not be lost.

As I sort through the unsettledness of being young and tired in an old and tired world, I don't understand how the losses pooled at my grandfather's feet could lead to faith, or how the same verses I learned from index cards have lived to be mature and seasoned in his soul.

I do not know yet in the way my grandfather does how God is present in the crushing empty hours. But it is my grandfather, and Mrs. Wrobbel, who teach me that we each have a liturgy to our lives, the verses we once read, the truth someone spoke into us, the songs woven through our childhood. *Shout for joy to the* LORD*, all the earth.* This is a liturgy too strong to be broken, the glass fitting into our empty places. *Know that the* LORD *is God, it is he who made us, and we are his.*

I told Mrs. Wrobbel years later that I still think of her when I open to the Psalms. She giggled. "Really?" She is shaky and pieced together and standing with every loss that has shaped her and every Scripture she has carried. *For the* LORD *is good and his love endures forever; his faithfulness continues through all generations.*

We come as children or we come not at all. And one day I will discover my soul like an infant finding her toes, feel mortal pains groan out of me. I will stretch into the truest silence, watch every longing fall shiny from its casing. I will be stripped, birthed, curled into the hand of God.

Many people have supported me in writing this book; I am grateful to the crowd of friends and family who have surrounded me.

In particular, I would like to thank Lil Copan, an amazingly gifted editor, whose questions, changes, interest, and friendship have helped carve this book. Thank you.

Miriam Blank and Dan Miller, who came into my life at just the right time.

Kirsten Kamm, who prays generously for me and those I love.

My sister, Dorie, who is such an important part of these childhood memories and who always let me be "Laura" when we played Little House on the Prairie.

And especially Eric, who has helped me with every word, who holds me up and laughs with me and loves me. I love coming home to you.

INTRODUCTION

p. xii "all the people gave a great shout. . . . " Ezra 3:11

p. xii "wept aloud when they saw the foundation of this temple being laid. . . . " Ezra 3:12

p. xii "no one could distinguish the sound of the shouts of joy. . . . " Ezra 3:13

CHAPTER THREE

All That Might Be: Hope

p. 29 "My soul is downcast within me. . . ." Lamentations 3:20b–22

CHAPTER SIX

The Missing Hours: Time and Opportunity

p. 62 "So what do people get. . . . " Ecclesiastes 2:22 (NLT)

CHAPTER SEVEN

Jumping In: Courage

p. 72 "Now faith is being sure of what we hope for. . . . " Hebrews 11:1

CHAPTER EIGHT

One Thing: Passion

p. 86 The story of the woman pouring perfume on Jesus' feet: Luke 7:36–38

CHAPTER NINE

First Words: Voice

p. 96 "A voice says, 'Cry out!'. . . ." Isaiah 40:6

CHAPTER ELEVEN

And Heaven to Earth Will Answer: God

p.115 "Enter his gates with thanksgiving. . . . " Psalm 100:4

p.116 "I will instruct you and teach you. . . . " Psalm 32:8

p.117 "Your path led through the sea, . . . " Psalm 77:19

p.118 "All my longings. . . . " Psalm 38:9

p.120 "The LORD is good, a strong hold. . . . " Nahum 1:7 (KJV)

p.121 "Shout for joy. . . . " Psalm 100:1

p.122 "Know that the LORD is God. . . . " Psalm 100:3

p.122 "For the LORD is good, and his love endures. . . . " Psalm 100:5